BUILDING BOUNCE®

WITH KIDS

A FAITH BASED TRAUMA-INFORMED APPROACH TO
BUILDING RESILIENT KIDS
STEFANIE HINMAN

Endorsements

"If you could only have one book about family and raising children, this book should be it! In *Building Bounce with Kids,* Stefanie lays out amazingly helpful principles for building healthy family relationships and children with strong emotional capacity. Even if you don't have kids, you should still read this—it will help *you* learn how to build capacity for *yourself!*"

—Dr. Bill Atwood, Anglican Bishop
Bishop of International Diocese Anglican Church of North America,
Author of *The General, The Boy, and Recapturing Joy*

"Stefanie Hinman has written a must-read primer for anyone desiring to better understand the effects of childhood trauma, and better yet, what to do about it. Whether you're a parent, a child worker, or someone who has survived childhood abuse or trauma, Stefanie breaks it down in easy to understand terms, then provides step-by-step guidance on practical ways to overcome and build resilience. This is not just a quick read, it is a resource, and perhaps a life raft for some."

—Rick Braschler, Kanakuk Kamps
Director of Safety and Risk, Kanakuk Kamps

"Anyone working in the field of trauma care will benefit from Stefanie's insights and experience, but most importantly, *Building Bounce with Kids* is a readable resource for every mom and dad."

—Ken R. Canfield, PH.D,
President & Founder National Center for Fathering

"In Building Bounce with Kids, Stefanie brings complex psychology down to earth with simple word pictures, powerful analogies, and practical steps and exercises for putting these powerful lessons to work in the lives of the kids you work with."

—Michael Sullivant, Author
Author, Pastor, Speaker,
Director of Relational Networks Life Model Works

"*Building Bounce with Kids* is perfect for parents, caregivers, teachers, and anyone who works with kids. Whether this is your first or fourth book on resilience, this is likely to become your new favorite. If you are looking for a church program, look no further. This book provides the education and the exercises you need to not only help the kiddos, but the parents as well."

—Kim Jones, Christian Life Coach
Founder of Restoration Pathways, LLC

"This book sheds light on a critical topic in child and youth discipleship: how to speak to kids who have experienced significant trauma or neglect. So many practical tools have been mined out of Stefanie's years of experience and gathered together here in one excellent book!"

—Matt Adams, Young Life
Strategic Initiatives Director Young Life Europe

"Whether you work with kids or have kids of your own, Stefanie's experience and insight will give you the tools to love those children well. And in the end, I expect it may even bring breakthroughs to parts of your own life."

—Meghan Adams, Artist, Mom
Artist, Mom, YoungLife Volunteer

"Stefanie's principles and exercises have been tested and proven through her work with trauma over the years, and her compassion and expertise are a powerful combo. I highly recommend this book to parents and therapists alike!"

—Terri Sullivant,
Co-pastor New Hope Community, Founder of Fully Alive Coaching,
Author of *The Divine Invitation: Entering the Dance of Becoming Fully Alive*

"I have learned a lot from Stefanie Hinman both about building resilience and working with kids. Her new book provides a fascinating look into the minds and hearts of children and offers helpful models and practical solutions for attuning to their needs and growing their resilience. This book will help everyone who reads it, even if they don't work directly with children."

—Dr. Marcus Warner, President, Deeper Walk International,
Co-author of Building Bounce: How to Grow Emotional Resilience

"There are many books I have read, but few which have had a lasting impact on me like this one. As a parent and as a leader, the wisdom of these pages are a treasure. This is an essential guidebook for one of the major challenges of our time. The blend of sociology, theory, leadership principles and is a wonderful mix, and the practical steps and processes that are offered can bring an authentic engagement with the message. The book leaves me inspired to be different but also, with instruction on how to change myself, and help others to change. I cannot recommend this book highly enough."

-Rich Robinson
Catalyst and Coach
Catalyst Change

Stefanie Hinman, M.S., ATR-BC, BCCC

Copyright © 2021 by Stefanie Hinman All rights reserved. No part of this publication may be reproduced, stored in any retrieval system, or transmitted in any form or by any means—electronic, mechanical, photocopy, recording, or any other—except for brief quotations in reviews, without the prior permission of the publisher.

All rights reserved worldwide. ISBN-13: 979-8985625592

Content Editor: Holden Hill

Edited by Calley Overton

Cover design: Scott Soliz

Printed in the United States of America

For the Children

Contents

Preface 13

Chapter One: My Story: An Excerpt from Building Bounce . . . 21

Chapter Two: Understanding Trauma 35

Chapter Three: Building Joy Base Camp 49

Chapter Four: Bouncing Back: Navigate Emotions 79

Chapter Five: Bouncing Back: Calm and Refill 105

Chapter Six: Power of Story 135

Chapter Seven: Some Joy Before You Go 155

Resources for Further Study 159

Preface

My very first job out of college, I worked at a home for children with behavior disorders. Most of the children who lived in this home were in the foster care system but couldn't stay in their placements due to the severity of their disruptive behavior. On my very first week, I met a spunky little girl who forever changed my perspective as a caregiver.

On my first day of training, the dorm leader training me shook her head with an exhausted look on her face. "You can't love these kids whole," she said. "You people come in here thinking you're gonna love these kids whole, and you get eaten alive." Maybe she could smell my naiveté, maybe she was hardened from years of working in difficult situations, or maybe she was right. But by the end of that first day, I had met my first teacher: a cute seven-year-old girl named Ava.[1*]

Ava was the toughest, meanest, most intimidating child I had ever come across. She was queen bee of the twelve-child dorm. No one befriended anyone in the dorm without Ava's stamp of approval. After lunch, Ava began to escalate for reasons unknown. Her rising agitation was met swiftly by a consequence from the dorm leader: Ava lost the privilege of going to the pool with the rest of the kids.

---

[1] * Names and details changed.

She began to melt down. With a slew of curse words, Ava became aggressive with the other children. Then she did it. I wasn't sure at first what happened or why it received the reaction it did, but Ava bit one of the other kids and the whole dorm jumped into action. The kids all went crazy, the dorm leader called for backup, and three large men came in and began the Mandt System protocol on this forty-pound child.

For those not familiar with Mandt, it is a way of physically restraining a child who threatens harm to self or others. It took three large men to restrain this little girl, and it wasn't easy. I watched as she outwitted and outmatched them for what felt like twenty minutes. The men finally prevailed. They placed her in a special, padded room where she could do herself no harm. She would remain isolated and alone until she calmed down.

My coworker, reading the horror on my face, pulled out a stack of files from a file cabinet and plopped them in front of me. "You should know the stories of the kids you're working with," she said, and then she left the room. I spent the next couple hours reading story after story of horrific physical, emotional, and sexual abuse. Police reports, social worker reports, and court records told the story of each child now in my care. Ava's mom was a prostitute who—when she was too high to perform—had pimped out her daughter. I now understood why it took three men to get her into a proper Mandt restraint. She knew how to kick and claw her way out of just about any situation. And the fact that she was potentially HIV positive explained what all the fuss was about when she started biting the other kids. Biting was her most powerful weapon, and she knew it.

Why do I tell you this story? Because I never forgot the powerlessness I felt in those moments. I have spent twenty-five years asking questions posed by that incident and the countless others that have followed. Knowing what I know today, I realize that every time those men had to physically restrain that little girl, it retraumatized her brain and body. At the time, restraining her was all we knew to do to protect her and everyone around her. But today we understand a lot more about the neurobiology of trauma. We understand more about dysregulation. We know how to speak to the emotional brain and use nonverbal cues to calm the body before the child escalates into fight, flight, or freeze (FFF) and becomes a threat to themselves or others. I have wished many times that I could go back and use what I know now with those children from my past. What if we could have better attuned to Ava's agitation? Could we have asked better questions about why her nervous system was feeling unsafe? Could we have sent nonverbal safety cues to her system instead? Could we have de-escalated the situation before she flipped her lid? Would that have changed the outcome? These are all questions, terms, and concepts that we will unpack together in this book.

I have no idea what happened to Ava or where she is today. But I have spent years working with adult survivors of complex childhood trauma. I have seen how unresolved grief and trauma form complex layers of physical, emotional, spiritual, and relational consequences. I have made it my mission to discover how to mitigate the effects of trauma in a young person early enough that they are not sentenced to a life of addiction, broken relationships, and suffering. None of the children from my years of work asked for the circumstances that shaped them, but shape them they did.

In my first five years as an art therapist in both foster care and hospice settings, the children I worked with had seen more adversity, trauma, and loss in their few years than most people experience in a lifetime. I often found myself wondering if our best practices of care were really helping. I could work for hours with a child on emotional expressiveness or learning to feel safe. However, if the family system or community culture around them was emotionally unsafe, the child would be punished for expressing their emotions or, worse, retraumatized by the adults in their lives who were stuck in dysfunctional patterns of relating. I learned that children heal and grow best in family systems and community cultures that give them the physical, emotional, and spiritual nutrients they need.

Even though I often felt discouraged in those early years, I began asking one crucial question:

Why do some kids bounce back, or even bounce forward, after adversity and some get stuck in it?

Because of my work with children facing adversity, I was asked to help create a resilience-building program for children who have a family member with a chronic illness. This request began my twenty-year search for answers to this one question. This question still drives me as a mom and a therapist today.

Until this point, researchers had studied what made adults resilient but had not really delved into what made children resilient. This question became the focus of my research and work, but it was motherhood that became the most motivating factor in my search for finding how to equip children to thrive in a world filled with adversity. In child after child and family after family, patterns began to emerge. Certain key factors create strong, healthy families, and strong, healthy families create strong, healthy kids.

After years of study and practice, I learned a few truths that I consider very good news:

1. No matter how old you are, you can learn to become more resilient.
2. The more resilient you are, the more resilient the children who depend on you will become.
3. There are ways to mitigate trauma and to enter into the life of a child and help them heal so that they do not carry unresolved trauma and grief into their adult life.

Building Bounce by Marcus Warner and me focuses on the first two truths: helping families build more capacity and resilience. This resource, *Building Bounce with Kids*, is a trauma-informed companion resource for teaching specific resilience-building skills to children and specifically focuses on number three.

This resilience model is rooted in the kind of secure attachment that builds joy. The best kind of secure attachment happens when families have the skills to form healthy bonds, are able to attune well to one another (listen and connect), and can stay relational in the face of challenges. Unfortunately, many people were not taught this kind of secure attachment. The good news is that it takes only one caring, attuned adult to teach a child resilience. I have heard many children who come from difficult pasts say that it was a teacher or grandparent who believed in them and taught them they were valuable.

Sadly, our world seems to be increasing in adversity and decreasing in authentic joy. In the book *Living from the Heart Jesus Gave You*, Friesen, Wilder, Bierling, Koepcke, and Poole detail the developmental tasks each person must complete to become a mature adult. Yet according to Dr. Jim Wilder, a large percentage of adults haven't completed them. He indicates that many men and women still in infant or child-level maturity are managing families, jobs, and ministries. When maturity-tasks are left unlearned, adults develop anxiety, depression, or unhealthy coping strategies like addictions, exploding in anger, or shutting down. Also, because parents cannot teach what they do not know, children then do not learn the developmental emotional maturity tasks they need to navigate their emotions well.

Dr. Diana Fosha says, "Aloneness in the face of overwhelming emotion is the epicenter of emotional suffering," and "Attachment is the key to undoing aloneness." The first step to healing is "undoing aloneness." This does not mean that kids who have secure attachments will not experience trauma, but it does mean that the unconditional love and support of healthy attachment is powerful in helping a child find healing and restoration after experiencing trauma.

In my work with complex-trauma survivors, an absence of caring, attuned adults seems to have created their deepest level of pain. We call this pain "attachment pain." Attachment pain is the gut-wrenching hurt of feeling abandoned and alone in a world that we feel unequipped to navigate. It is the feeling of belonging nowhere and having no one with whom to journey through our story. I have often heard stories of war veterans losing a limb during combat but having phantom pain where the limb used to be. This is how I see attachment pain. We have a God-given need to be loved and accepted for who we are without fear of rejection. When this need is unmet, it leaves a phantom pain in the place where love was supposed to be that seems to hurt even worse than the direct wounds caused by those who are supposed to love us.

If you are an adult who still feels the haunting pain of attachment wounds, I have good news: Jesus came to heal the brokenhearted and set the captive free. He can enter into your deepest places of pain with a love that heals. I have provided a list of resources for emotional healing from attachment pain in the back of this book.

This book will focus on equipping adults to enter the life of a child in a way that builds joy bonds and teaches the child to navigate the ups and downs of life. If the children in your life have had trauma, you can help mitigate it so they don't get stuck in unhealthy emotional states or patterns. Thankfully not all children have a trauma history like Ava's, but all children will experience adversity. This resource will help you teach skills to children that increase their resilience. It is for all families and not just those with trauma history. I have spent years teaching these principles to many diverse organizations and families. They are time tested and they work.

Chapter One

My Story: An Excerpt from Building Bounce

When my children were little, I spent a lot of time and energy trying to protect them from germs. I would wipe down grocery carts and restaurant tables. I would have them wash their hands after preschool or time spent in the church nursery. I could feel my anxiety rise when other moms talked about the latest virus or strep going around. I was tired of the constant anxiety I felt about my children's safety, so I asked the Lord about it. That's when this thought dropped into my head: I needed to shift my focus. Instead of trying to protect them from every threat that might come their way, I needed to focus on building their immune systems. This way, when (not *if*) the germs came their way, they would have the strength to fight them. This thought brought me peace, and I immediately felt my breathing grow deeper and my shoulders relax. The idea of building my children's immune systems felt way more manageable than trying to eradicate every germ from their lives.

Building bounce is a lot like building your body's immune system. Instead of avoiding emotions and the situations that cause them, we want to learn how to deal with them and bounce back so we feel like ourselves more quickly.

One day my daughter got in the car after school. With tears in her eyes, she told me that a little girl she tried to play with at recess had run away from her. Her pain broke my heart. I started a quiet rant at God for allowing this to happen.

However, I felt the Father's gentle words straight to my heart: "Do you trust me with Taylor's heart?"

"Yes, Lord, but she feels rejected. We all know how painful that is."

He replied, "Yes, for a moment Taylor felt rejected, but I never left her side, and today she learned compassion." He then reminded me of how butterflies must struggle as they break free from their chrysalis. If not allowed to struggle, the butterfly will not develop the wing strength to fly. The Lord asked me to trust him with my daughter's heart. He knows who he created her to be and exactly what she needs to experience to grow into that beautiful and strong young woman.

I wanted to emotionally bubble wrap my children to protect them from adversity. God wanted to use the adversity to strengthen their resilience. My job at that moment was to attune to my daughter's pain, let her know that I was with her, and speak truth to her about her value and beauty. This was the first of many lessons God would teach me about trusting him with my children.

As with building their immune systems, my focus has shifted from protecting my kids from adversity to now preparing them for it and walking with them in it. We know that in this life there will be many trials. It's not an *if*, but a *when*. We cannot control the hardships our children face, but we can help build their resilience and emotional capacity so that when they face it, they have the strength and tools to not just bounce back but grow even stronger.

This book is about building bounce. Below is a quick overview of terms and concepts we will unpack in the chapters that follow.

What Is Bounce?

Bounce is our ability to bounce back from adversity. It's also known as our "emotional capacity" or "resilience." We will use these terms somewhat interchangeably.

Emotional capacity is like an emotional immune system. The stronger it is, the better we rebound from adversity. It could also be thought of as our ability to carry weight. The more capacity we have, the more weight we can carry.

We can learn to bounce forward. "Posttraumatic growth" refers to our ability to grow our emotional capacity after facing adversity.

Capacity Bubble

The term capacity bubble is used to imagine what our capacity looks like. Everyone has a capacity bubble. It's kind of like our skin. It keeps the good stuff in and the bad stuff out.

We are born without a developed capacity bubble. Ideally, it gets developed in our first few years of life. All the relational joy we receive as we are enjoyed by our parents and grandparents fills our bubble with joy. Another analogy is a joy battery. Joy then gives us the strength to face the challenges of life.

Trauma, however, pokes holes in our capacity bubble. If trauma happens in our early years, before the bubble develops, the bubble will not form or will form incorrectly. The more holes a person has in their capacity bubble the harder it is to hold in the good stuff and keep out the bad stuff. If you do not have a bubble or your bubble has a lot of holes it will feel like no matter how hard people try, it never seems to fill the gaping hole in your desire to feel loved and the joy will leak faster than anyone can fill it. Thankfully when Jesus heals the trauma, he plugs the holes. Then you can learn to connect with God and others in ways that fill your capacity bubble with joy.

Why do some people bounce back from trauma and even seem to get stronger and some crumble? The answer is emotional capacity.

Our capacity bubble grows just like a muscle. When we experience challenges, or suffering, just like going to the gym we may feel pain but we get stronger.

However, when a person doesn't have EC they will use coping strategies like addiction or dissociation to cope with the strong overwhelming emotions of life.

We all have an emotional capacity bubble. I see our emotional capacity like a basketball or a tire. The rubber wall is like our skin. It keeps the good stuff in and the bad stuff out. The air in our capacity bubble is relational joy. God created our brains to run on joy. When our bubble is full of relational joy, it's bouncy and able to bounce back from adversity. When our bubble is low on relational joy, our ability to bounce back lessens.

Road Hazards: Slow Leaks, Triggers and Flats

Three road hazards that we need to learn to identify and navigate are leaks, triggers, and flats.

Slow Leaks

Our world is stressful. Healthy stress helps us grow while toxic stress makes us sick. Toxic stress is often rooted in traumatic events from childhood. These experiences disrupt healthy brain development and are associated with lifelong health and social problems. When childhood traumas go unresolved, they continue to affect us into adulthood. Thankfully, we can learn to resolve traumatic events so they don't follow us into adulthood. We can learn skills to help better manage stress so that it works for us and not against us.

Stress causes us to lose air in our capacity bubbles over a period of time. We call this kind of depletion "slow leaks." Just as with a leaky tire, driving through life with a low-pressure capacity bubble can be dangerous. But we can learn to detect a low joy level and gain skills to replenish it before it's too late.

"Self-replenishment" refers to detecting when we have lost air and having the skills to replenish the air supply. We will discuss self-replenishment and stress management in the self-care section (Chapter 5).

Triggers

If traumatic experiences remain unprocessed and unresolved, the emotions and sensory information from those experiences store in the brain and body unresolved. When this happens, those emotions and sensory input may remain active and continue to affect how we see the world and respond to stress. We call these "triggers." Sometimes we have narrative memory to explain our reactions and sometimes we do not.

Often toxic stress is fueled by triggers. Knowing our triggers and learning skills to return back to calm when we have been triggered helps prevent stress from turning toxic.

Karen sought counseling after experiencing a sudden onset of severe anxiety and panic attacks. She had no idea where the anxiety was coming from. The counselor began asking questions about Karen's activities and circumstances near the time of the first attack. Karen's face suddenly registered surprise. She said, "Oh my gosh, I can't believe I didn't see it. We had just celebrated my daughter's sixth birthday. I was six when my mother died!"

Bill couldn't stand his birthday. Bill's new wife tried hard to make this one special for him. She worked all day cooking a special dinner. She was devastated when, instead of being happy, he exploded in anger. After seeing how much pain he had caused his wife, Bill confessed that his dad walked out on his family on Bill's seventh birthday. The family didn't see him again for several years. Every year on his birthday, he relives the pain from that day.

Triggers can result from the unresolved grief or trauma of a specific event, or from coping strategies a person adopts in order to survive ongoing adverse conditions.

Sarah is a sweet little girl, but she hyperfocuses on being in control. When she is told no or is stopped from obtaining a goal, she melts down and becomes aggressive. Part of this overreactive behavior stems from Sarah's past. She spent her first few years living with her birth mother, who was an addict. Some days Sarah had food, and some days she did not. Some days her mom engaged with her, and sometimes her mom slept all day. The unpredictability of those years caused Sarah to fear unpredictability. She adapted her strategy of hypervigilance and control to try to manage the anxiety she felt.

After her adopted parents recognized that her behaviors come from a need for predictability and an assurance of safety, they were able to create a plan. They structured Sarah's day so that Sarah could predict what came next. They started a routine of rehearsing the day with Sarah every morning at breakfast. When the plan got disrupted, they helped Sarah learn to adapt and adjust without melting down. The more trust Sarah developed around her parents' stability, the easier it was for her to lay down her strategies of hypervigilance and control.

Some people who experience the death of a loved one report that every year around the anniversary of the loss, the sights, smells, and memories from the experience become intense and vivid. They remember details they had previously forgotten. We may not always be able to connect what we are feeling in the present with trauma from our past, but our body keeps score and will always be trying to heal. For more information on unresolved trauma read *The Body Keeps the Score* by Bessel van der Kolk.

Carol is a sixty-year-old grandmother of six. She came in for counseling because she felt extremely depressed and had despair she couldn't resolve. She reported, "I always struggle this time of year, but this year seems much worse." After we investigated further, Carol was able to connect her emotional state back to a miscarriage she had in her twenties. Every year around the time of the miscarriage, Carol felt the grief. Her body was remembering even though Carol was consciously unaware.

Triggers are felt in the present but embedded in the past. It's as if the emotional and sensory data from the experience gets buried alive in our mind and body. When something in the present reminds us of the past, this data triggers like a landmine. It floods our bodies with the stress hormones, emotions, and even the sensory information from the original event as though it is a fresh assault. Since getting triggered happens as a result of an unconscious system, we may have no knowledge of why we feel the intense emotion. And while getting triggered can happen in an instant, resolving the emotions and burning through the stress hormones takes time.

Trigger Demonstration for Kids: Find a Mason jar. Fill it with water and either dirt or glitter, depending on your preference. Place the jar on a table and let the contents settle until it looks like just a jar of clear water. Talk about how easy it is to see through the jar when the water is clear. Then, shake the jar and watch the dirt (or glitter) fly. Talk about how this is what happens to us when we get triggered. Discuss how it is hard to see clearly through the jar now. Becoming triggered affects our perceptions. Set the jar on the counter so that the kids can watch how long it takes for the dirt to settle back down. It takes time for the hormones that are released when we get triggered to settle down, too. We will learn skills to help burn off the stress hormones in Chapter 5.

Flats

If we have the skills to handle the stress, we are able to bounce back to homeostasis, our stable emotional condition. If we lack the emotional capacity to handle the stress, we may get stuck in a fight, flight, or freeze response (FFF). This threshold of going from stress to trauma is called "window of tolerance."

Dr. Daniel Siegal coined this term, "window of tolerance," to describe an individual's optimal functioning zone where they are best able to think, relate to others, and process new information. When a child becomes overwhelmed or overstimulated, they move outside of this optimal functioning zone. The child becomes either hyperaroused (highly emotional, dysregulated, or experiencing fight, flight, or sensory overload) or hypoaroused (withdrawn, numb, lack of emotion, reduced physical movement, or experiencing shutdown). When a person is outside of the window of tolerance, the mind and body will be unable to integrate all that happens in the moment or process new information.[2] This is referred to as being in a "state of dysregulation."

In Bounce terms, stress eventually builds to the point that we no longer have the skills to handle it. When we are pushed to the edge

---

2   Daniel J. Siegel, *The Developing Mind* (New York: Gilford, 1999).

of our emotional capacity bubble, the pressure blows a hole in the wall. Now we have a flat tire. If stress strains the capacity bubble wall beyond its pressure tolerance, you get a flat. This is trauma. The tire can no longer hold air and needs attention. Good news: we can learn to fix a flat.

The Two Types of Flats

The Life Model trauma recovery model defines two main types of flats helpful to this conversation: trauma A and trauma B. Trauma A is the absence of the good things we need to grow and mature. This includes neglect, having basic needs unmet, and the absence of healthy attachment or healthy relational skills needed to create belonging and connection. The second type of trauma is Trauma B. Trauma B is the presence of bad things. This kind is what we typically think of when we think of trauma: physical, emotional, and sexual abuse; car accidents; death of a loved one; and war.[3]

Type B trauma is usually easy to see. Type A is often hidden. All the time, I hear people say, "I never experienced abuse or anything traumatic as a child, but I still really struggle in some areas." Often, they missed developmental milestones because of an absence of something they needed. In fact, most if not all of us have gaps in our development. We can benefit from identifying those gaps and going

---

3   James G. Friesen et al., *Living from the Heart Jesus Gave You,* 15th Anniversary Study ed. (East Peoria, IL: Shepherd's House, 2016), 83–89.

back to learn what we missed as a child. Emotional capacity can also be called "emotional maturity." The more mature we are, the more weight we can carry.

I have worked with many adult survivors of childhood trauma. Many of them have had years of counseling and healing ministry and can't figure out why they still struggle so much. It is often because most of their counseling has focused on their type B trauma, but they also have type A. *Building Bounce*, the book I wrote with Marcus Warner, is a resource for bringing awareness to these type A traumas and provides tools for learning what was previously missed.

How Do We Build Bounce?

When we have slow leaks, triggers, and flats, how do we build or rebuild our bounce? There are three essential steps:

1. Build a joy base camp through relational connections that act as anchors for a state of feeling safe, calm, and connected (SCC). This step is related to secure attachment and emotional capacity (Chapter 3).
2. Build skills and pathways back to base camp after experiencing overwhelming emotions. We call this process "Building Bounce" (Chapter 4–5).
3. Bring awareness to the stories we believe (Chapter 6).

This book, *Building Bounce with Kids,* is a parent/caregiver resource for teaching these skills to children. Based on my years of studying what makes people more resilient and teaching emotional IQ to children, I firmly believe that these principles prepare children emotionally so that when adversity comes, they have the social support and emotional capacity to bounce forward instead of being crushed. *Building Bounce with Kids* is a trauma-informed resource and addresses how to teach the Building Bounce skills with children who have had trauma as well as those who have not.

Building relational skills to connect authentically with God, learning to know our own heart and connect authentically with others, and learning to cope with our emotions and return to joy are among the skills that we will address in this resource. We know from neuroscience that we must learn to return to joy from each of life's big emotions (shame, anger, disgust, sadness, fear, and hopeless despair—discussed further in Chapter 4). When these skills are not learned in childhood, an individual may struggle with fear and anxiety, turn to drugs and alcohol, become easily triggered, or just shut down. However, we can work with our kids to develop well-worn pathways so they learn skills to navigate their more overwhelming emotions. These skills will help prevent a lifetime of consequences from unhealthy coping strategies.

As parents, we cannot teach what we do not know. We can all benefit from identifying where we need new skills or reinforcement. Waking up to the truth of our own stories can be difficult, but it's so worth it. The Building Bounce process is really about developing the emotional capacity to grow, mature, and thrive.

But before we jump in, we must first discuss trauma and how our trauma history impacts the process of Building Bounce.

Chapter Two

Understanding Trauma

What Is Trauma?

Trauma can be defined as any experience that overwhelms a person to the degree that they believe they don't have the internal or external resources to bounce back from it.

To understand trauma, we must first understand the autonomic nervous system (ANS). If our ANS perceives a threat, the amygdala will sound the alarm, take over, and initiate FFF (fight, flight, or freeze).

FFF is a natural biological reaction to feeling overwhelmed. The amygdala is part of the brain and works like a fire alarm. When it perceives danger, the alarm bells go off. The ANS takes over and dumps stress hormones like cortisol and adrenaline into the body to give it increased energy to respond to the crisis. The natural response to a threat is to fight or flee (flight). If neither response is perceived as possible, a person will freeze or shut down. FFF happens to everyone. Our bodies are equipped to recover quickly and repair themselves from the flood of hormones. In the case of severe or prolonged trauma, however, an individual can become stuck in FFF and is then not able to return to a state of perceived safety.

What Does FFF Look Like in Children?

Fight. Fight looks like hitting, kicking, and yelling. The story of Ava from the preface is an example of fight. Ava was a fighter. She fought everyone about everything as a way of staying hypervigilant to danger.

Flight. Flight looks like running away, changing the subject, or distracting behaviors. I have had many "runners" come through my resilience classes. They are the class clowns, always dodging and weaving around the activities and discussions. They would rather start a paint war than talk about feelings or tell personal stories. They also often have super tender hearts, and dodging uncomfortable conversations is their survival strategy. If they let themselves feel the pain, they believe they might not have what they need to come back from it. I'm often amazed at the insights I hear from these young people once they have built trust to feel they are safe talking about their situation and have learned a few skills for bouncing back.

Freeze. Researchers are now identifying freeze and shutdown as separate biological responses to trauma. Both can look like zoning out, dissociating, crying, whining, or looking confused or scared. The difference is that freeze is a hypoarousal response and shutdown is an arousal response. Detecting freeze or shutdown may be more difficult. Children in these responses can look like they are paying attention, but inside they are frozen or shut down. They work hard to avoid being called on or attracting attention. They may even respond to direct questions, but their answer will most likely be what they think you want to hear. Inside they are checked out, thinking about other things or even on a vacation in their imagination. I will give more examples of this in Chapter 4.

Is Trauma the Same for Everyone?

What's traumatic for one person might not be traumatic for another. Capacity and experience affect what feels traumatic. A child who had a starvation experience at an orphanage may perceive losing snack time as traumatic because the ANS signals the body that it's in danger of starving, while skipping a snack for a child who has never gone hungry is less likely to trigger the ANS. And of course, there are differing levels of trauma. Falling and breaking an arm is a different kind of trauma than chronic abuse. Neglect, which is the absence of good things and a type A trauma, can be as traumatic as abuse, a type B trauma. Varying degrees of trauma will have varying degrees of effects on the mind, body, and spirit.

Trauma and Dysregulation

A primary symptom of trauma is difficulty regulating emotions. Children who have had trauma easily become dysregulated. We will discuss in Chapter 3 ways to teach children how to return to perceived safety after they have been triggered. The bottom line is that everyone has experienced trauma. The good news is that, no matter what kind of trauma you or your child has endured, there is hope. Healing is possible. Skills can be learned to help navigate a pathway from the trauma state back to a state of love and safety.

Consider this scenario: It's a beautiful sunny day. You and your child decide to saddle the horses to go on a trail ride. Suddenly your child's horse gets spooked by a snake and takes off running. You panic and chase after the horse that just hijacked your child. When you catch up to the horse, you recognize that the animal is spooked. So you calmly dismount your horse, take a deep breath, approach your child's horse, and grab it by the reins. You speak in a way that will reassure both the child and her horse that everything is going to be OK before you reach up and take your child back.

Dr. Bessel van der Kolk, in his book, *The Body Keeps the Score*, uses this rider and horse analogy to represent the relationship between two distinct functions of the brain.[4] The snake represents whatever

---

4   Bessel van der Kolk, *The Body Keeps Score: Brain, Mind, and Body in the*

perceived threat (real or imagined) the child may be experiencing. The horse represents the emotional brain and the rider represents the thinking/rational brain. The emotional brain takes over during the FFF response with overwhelming reactions like fear and anger. The thinking brain (the rider) is in charge of thinking, planning, decision-making, problem solving, reasoning, logic, and language. When the emotional brain hijacks your child, all of these higher-thinking parts of the brain go off-line. Siegal calls this off-line state "flipping the lid." You can try to reason with the child all you want, but the alarm bells in their head will be louder than you.

Flipping the Lid Demonstration

(For Teaching This Concept to Kids)

Siegal and Dr. Tina Payne Bryson use a hand exercise in *The Whole-Brain Child* to explain to children what happens when the snake from our analogy spooks the horse.

In this demonstration, the thumb represents the primitive "downstairs thinking" that includes the brain stem and the limbic regions. These regions are responsible for basic functions like breathing, fight, flight, and stronger emotions like anger and fear. The four fingers of the hand represent the "upstairs thinking" that is responsible for higher-order thinking. This includes analytical thinking, problem solving, language, thinking before acting, self-understanding, and considering

---

Healing of Trauma (New York: Penguin, 2015), 64.

how others feel.

When the upstairs and downstairs are working together (vertical integration), all the parts of the brain can communicate, cooperate, and send appropriate signals to the body. When an individual experiences overwhelming emotions that trigger the ANS, he or she will do what is called "flipping the lid" or "losing your mind."

Try this: make a fist around your thumb. This demonstrates vertical integration with full brain-body connection. Now, flip your hand open so that your four fingers are no longer making contact with your thumb. When this break happens in our brain, connection is lost between upstairs thinking and the downstairs thinking. The thinking brain (including the language centers) goes off-line, along with the individual's ability to think rationally. The emotional brain takes over, and the child (or adult) can feel hijacked.[5]

Going back to the horse analogy, when you see that a child (or adult) has "flipped their lid," the goal will be to communicate with the child's emotional brain (the horse) that they are safe and can calm back down.

Trauma and Learning Emotional Regulation

One big difference between you and the child in Van der Kolk's

---

5   Siegel and Bryson, *The Whole-Brain Child: 12 Revolutionary Strategies to Nurture Your Child's Developing Mind* (New York: Bantam Books, 2012), 62–63.

analogy is that you have a fully developed prefrontal cortex (PFC) and the child does not. The PFC is the mediator and communicator between the two brain functions. It's what allows us to integrate our thinking and feeling into a story that makes sense. Siegal and Bryson emphasize our need for both vertical and horizontal integration. Vertical integration refers to connecting the downstairs thinking (primitive brain responses) and the upstairs thinking (higher-order responses)—the connection that breaks during dysregulation. Horizontal integration assimilates the emotional/creative right brain and the thinking/logical left brain by naming feelings and expressing them in healthy ways (more in Chapter 4).

Since the PFC continues to mature well into our twenties, kids need adults to help them make sense of their experiences. We lend them our PFC until theirs is fully functioning. We help them tell the stories that allow them to integrate traumatic memory into a narrative they can process. Until the emotional and thinking brains learn to work together, they cannot see the whole picture. But we can.

Unfortunately, early childhood abuse and neglect negatively affect the development of integration and emotional regulation. So if the children you are working with have had trauma, you may need to give them more opportunities to catch up developmentally.

Ideally, children learn to regulate emotions through a process of external regulation and co-regulation (Chapter 5). This means that in healthy development, a child will have hundreds of experiences of an attuned parent with a regulated nervous system meeting their needs and helping them to calm after distress. For example, when a baby cries, an attuned adult is able to identify with the baby's distress, meet the baby's need, soothe the baby, and help the baby return to feeling safe, calm, and connected (SCC). This builds pathways in the brain from the big emotions back to a state of SCC.

When you are working with children who have had trauma, however, it will be necessary to understand that this process has been disrupted. Children with traumatic histories often become easily dysregulated. They might even remain in a continuous state of FFF. But it is possible to help them heal from trauma's effects. By providing high-connection and high-sensory environments and experiences, you help build the connections in their brains they need to learn how to better co-regulate and self-regulate their emotions and return to SCC.[6] The TBRI® website offers many wonderful resources for building such an environment. Also, my organization, Healing Expressions, has created three high connection and high-sensory children's programs designed to help teach the resiliency skills taught in this book. The programs are available at healingexpressionskc.com.

Each time you help a child move from a state of dysregulation (overwhelmed) to a state of feeling connected and safe through co-regulation, you build pathways they can use to better self-regulate in the

---

6   Siegel and Bryson, *Whole-Brain Child*.

future. The more the pathways are used, the stronger they will become, and eventually the child will be able to navigate it on their own.

Concerning Dysregulation and Discipline

Imagine with me that your thirteen-year-old daughter just got home from school. You ask her if she can take the trash out. She seems noticeably upset. She ignores you and walks toward her bedroom. You raise your voice a little and ask her again. This time, she screams, "Why don't you do it yourself!" before thundering into her room and slamming the door.

What do you do? Option 1: Kick your daughter's door down, ask her just who she thinks she is, and ground her for the week. Option 2: Enter her room gently, take her hand or give her a hug to calm her down, and ask what's wrong.

If you guessed option 2, you are correct.

It's tempting to see this state of dysregulation as a discipline issue. But dysregulation is *not* a discipline issue. It is also easy to become triggered by our children's disrespectful behavior and act out of our emotional brain. Often, the emotional overreactions we see in our children are the result of a child feeling overwhelmed. If our child has flipped their lid, they are acting out of their emotional brain. We can lovingly attune to them in the moment, ask questions about what happened at school to make them feel overwhelmed, and communicate that they are not alone. Chances are that once your child feels heard and seen, they will start to calm down, share about the day, allow you to speak truth into their experience, and return to SCC. Once the child is feeling like themself again, it is always good to circle back around and address the inappropriate behaviors.

The general principle is to keep the relationship bigger than the problem or conflict. When children are able to rupture and repair in a safe, joy-bonded relationship, they will build stronger pathways back from overwhelming emotions to SCC.

When a child has had a lot of trauma, this process is a bit more complicated. Trauma can alter brain development, sensory processing, and neurochemistry, and can negatively impact a child's ability to embrace secure attachment. It is very possible to build bounce with a child who has had trauma but it will be a more complicated process. Dysfunctional patterns of behavior are often driven by fear, pain, and unmet needs. Therefore, seeking to understand what needs the child is trying to meet and finding creative ways to help the child better meet those needs will have a more successful outcome than disciplining for the behavior. Don't get me wrong, there is certainly a time for discipline. But trying to use discipline when a child is already dysregulated is like pouring fuel on a fire, and it often drives the child into feeling alone in their overwhelmed state. For further information, the book *The Connected Child* by Dr. Karyn Purvis offers helpful information on how to respond to dysregulation effectively.[7]

More and more research is emerging that shows the difference between suffering and trauma is whether or not we feel alone in our experience. Attunement is a skill that communicates to someone, "I am here with you in what you are experiencing and I have the emotional capacity to sit with you in your big emotion." As a mom, I look for ways to communicate to my children that life will have many ups and downs, but they are never alone. "God is always with you and I am here for you, too. We can do this together!"

There is much more to say on this topic of trauma than I can fit in one chapter. If you are a trauma survivor please know that Melissa Finger MS, NCC and I will be releasing *Building Bounce for Trauma Survivors* soon, because we understand that building bounce as a trauma survivor is a much more complicated journey. Visit Healingexpressionskc.com to stay informed on new releases.

Being Stretched

All kids will encounter adversity in some form, even those who never experience the harsh realities of abuse or neglect we often think of as trauma. Thankfully, neither trauma nor adversity have to define us, but both can lead to us and our children being stretched. "Being stretched" sounds about as fun as being pruned or refined by fire.

---

7   Karyn B. Purvis, David R. Cross, and Wendy Lyons Sunshine, *The Connected Child: Bring Hope and Healing to Your Adoptive Family* (New York: McGraw-Hill, 2007).

However, just like scripture teaches, God often uses adversity to grow us. In this instance, "being stretched" refers to when we are sitting on the edge of our emotional capacity bubble and are practicing recovery skills. This practice allows the walls of our capacity bubble to stretch, enlarging our window of tolerance and allowing for growth.

The edge of our emotional capacity may sound like a dangerous place; however, there is actually a hidden beauty in sitting on the edge of our capacity. I learned this truth while taking a Pilates class several years ago. Pilates, in case you haven't tried it, is an exercise system that works the small muscles in your body. As I was holding a crazy position that I'm sure God never intended for the human body, both of my legs started shaking uncontrollably. I wanted to quit, but the instructor yelled from the front, "Embrace the pain." The shaking was the goal. That is where strength building has its greatest potential. I was definitely sitting on the edge of my physical capacity!

Just like going to the gym and working our bodies to the point of sore muscles and exhaustion, when we are sitting on the edge of our emotional capacity and have the internal and external resources to recover, we grow stronger. When we're doing hard things—whether wrestling with God over a place in our story where we felt abandoned, asking forgiveness and engaging in conflict resolution with somebody we harmed, or acknowledging places where we need healing—we can rest in the truth that buried within this struggle is an opportunity for growth. Conflict plus resolution equals intimacy. Rupture plus repair equals greater strength.

Coming to the end of our emotional capacity and nursing our neural pathways back to joy actually strengthens our resiliency. This principle is essential to understand. When I speak on parenting, shame, and attachment, parents will come up to me and say something like, "I've totally messed this up, what do I do?" I always respond with the research.

Research shows that it's better to have a ruptured and repaired capacity bubble than to have never ruptured at all. I know this idea may sound counterintuitive, but there is a truth here that should encourage us. Dr. Curt Thompson says in his book *The Soul of Shame*, "Secure attachment is not primarily about the absence of pain but the presence of joy in the face of those challenging places. It is not about the absence of ruptures but the faithful repair of ruptures, even when repair seems beyond the reach of our imaginations."[8]

We often think that if we can protect our kids from all harm they will be better off, but the truth is that if we protect our kids from all struggles, they will miss out on opportunities to grow stronger. Even trees need storms and drought to grow strong. And let's face it, we live in a world with extreme adversity. But we have a God who is with us in it all.

---

8   Curt Thompson, *The Soul of Shame* (Downer's Grove, IL: InterVarsity, 2015), 53.

Please don't mistake what I'm saying to mean that as parents we need to go out and provide adversity for our kids. That is certainly *not* what I'm saying. Life will provide plenty of struggle for them. Our job is to walk with them and help them navigate it—loan them our emotional capacity so they know they are not alone. We can start by helping them build a joy base camp.

Chapter Three

Building Joy Base Camp

We learn more about the brain all the time. Brain scientists agree that healthy attachments are essential to good brain and nervous system development. Three ministries, Life Model Works, Deeper Walk International, and THRIVEtoday, have developed practical resources for understanding the neuroscience and power of joy and how to grow more joy by creating healthy attachments. They call these joy bonds. In their writings, "joy base camp" refers to having a well-developed joy center in the brain.[9]

Our brain was designed to run on joy. It's the air that gives us bounce. The joy center in the brain develops in a context of secure attachment with others. Secure attachments can also be referred to as having a "secure base" or a "firm foundation." It's what we recognize

---

9   Joy base camp is a Life Model concept. See Friesen et al., *Living from the Heart Jesus Gave You*, 74–81.

as "home." It's what grounds our hearts, minds, and nervous systems. Without a home, we have nowhere to return to after an adventure.

When I was sixteen, my family moved to a new city. I remember driving up to our new house for the first time, walking through the door, and asking, "Will this house ever feel like home?" The concept of "home" was very distinct and held much meaning, but I doubt I could have ever put its definition into words. Over a few weeks, the new house did indeed start to feel like home. Our family began doing all the things our family does. We ate together at the table, watched TV together in the evening, set up our own spaces that felt like us. I arranged my new room with all of the things from my old room. Each object held sentimental value and represented something that mattered to me. When I had the space the way I wanted, I sat back, looked around, and declared, "Now this feels like my room!" Before I had arranged it, it was just boring walls with boring carpet. Now with all my memories and sentiments hanging around, it felt like me. It had my trophies, stuffed animals, familiar lamp, furniture, bedspread, and pictures of my friends. We had started the process of re-creating home.

After establishing my room as base camp, it was time to learn my way around. It was summer time, so I first drove around with my parents and learned where the grocery store, gas station, and movie rental stores were. I drove around town with help long enough to have confidence that I could navigate on my own. One morning, I decided

I should venture out by myself. I will never forget getting in the car and saying to myself, "You can do this!" I wrote down every turn I made so I could find my way back home. My heart pounded. Since cell phones hadn't been invented yet, if I got lost I would have to stop and use a pay phone to get home.

Over time I figured out where the church and the high school were. The first few months, I made many wrong turns and even got lost. But I eventually found my way home with the help of a map. After about a year of living in this new city, I found that I no longer needed the map. In fact, I no longer needed to think about where I was. I could find my way home on autopilot while talking with a friend or singing to my favorite music.

This story is much like the process of building bounce. We first need to establish what a safe home looks and feels like, and then we can learn to return home from all of the adventures and emotions that make up a normal day in the life of me.

What Is Joy? Why Is It Important?

"From your brain's perspective, joy can be defined as relational happiness. Joy is the feeling of being with someone who is happy to be with me. Joy creates a twinkle in our eyes, a smile on our faces, and floods our bodies with positive energy."[10] Joy flows from connection.

---

10 Marcus Warner, *Building Bounce* (Carmel, IN: Deeper Walk International, 2020), 18.

Joy activates the brain's social engagement system and prepares us to engage with God and others.

As parents, laying a firm attachment foundation is key to teaching our children how to live in joy. Children who experience secure attachment in childhood are able to create connection and a sense of belonging later in life. If you are a parent looking to create secure attachments with your children but never experienced it yourself as a child, there is hope. It's never too late to learn.

How do we grow the joy center in our brains? By experiencing joy through healthy connections with others. Life Model calls these "joy bonds." The joy center is developed through hours of eye-to-eye and face-to-face interaction between baby and caregivers. I am convinced that parenthood is one of life's biggest capacity-building experiences. Nothing is as challenging and rewarding. When my children were babies, my husband and I spent hours staring at them, delighting in their every facial expression, and wondering what they were thinking. I will never forget the first time each one of them smiled at me. The joy I felt was almost more than I could take. I thought there was nothing better on earth—until I heard their first belly laughs.

According to Wilder, babies need countless hours of eye-to-eye delight and engagement for their joy center to develop fully. But joy in and of itself can be overwhelming if not placed within a rhythm of connection and rest. Babies love to find someone's eyes and squeal in delight, but they must also look away and rest so they do not become overwhelmed. When we can connect together and rest together, our brains get a complete joy workout.

Rhythms of Joy and Quiet

Joy bonding doesn't end in infancy. I continually look for ways to build joy bonds with my children. We hunt for opportunities that require phones be put down for eye-contact and joy-building moments. We play games, take trips, and go on hikes together, and I make sure that every time they walk in the door, my kids see that I'm happy they're home. We also look for ways to rest together and enjoy being still. Experiencing joy together produces dopamine and builds bonds; "quieting" together produces serotonin and builds trust in our bond.[11]

"Quieting" refers to quieting our heart, mind, and body, whether that happens at the end of a joy-filled day or an overwhelming day. We can quiet by sitting next to a loved one on the couch or going out on the back deck to sit in nature, take deep breaths, listen to the birds, and feel the breeze on our face. It's about becoming fully present in the moment, focusing on goodness, and taking time to connect with God and others. I have learned to attune to my own nervous system and the nervous system of my family. When I notice that the room is becoming intense, I will take deep breaths and calm my nervous system first.

---

11   Thrive International, *Building Bonds* webinar presented by Amy Brown, August 2020.

Just as we are always told when flying to put our oxygen mask on first so we are able to put the masks on our children, neurologically, calming ourselves first is required because only a regulated nervous system can offer co-regulation to another.

Sometimes putting on worship music, singing, or taking a quiet break helps too. When my kids were little, I would take breaks during the day for quieting. Even after my kids were done napping, we would have quiet time in the room or sit together and do a quiet activity.

Whether I'm at home with my family or working with kids in one of our resiliency classes, I will often start to feel the energy in the room begin to build. When the room starts to feel overwhelming, I like to stop and take a breathing break or mindful minute. When we're working with kids, this break often looks like a game. We will discuss quieting activities in more detail in the next chapter, but I thought it important to mention here since joy and quiet are two essential components of joy bonding.

Joy Bonding with Teenagers

I hear all the time that teenage boys are difficult to joy-bond with. I get it. My seventeen-year-old son is often uninterested in hanging out with me. I have to look for creative ways and opportunities to connect with him. Sometimes that means a simple pat on the shoulder as I walk by, sitting next to him on the couch quietly, asking him to play a game that I know he likes, or listening to his favorite music and singing along with him.

When he seems uninterested in spending time with me, I reassure myself that deep down he loves that I want to spend time with him. I look for occasions for eye contact and a smile. When he walks in the room, I light up and say, "Hey Buddy!" His brain will register the "she's happy to be with me" feeling even if he won't admit that he likes it. No matter what, I want my kids to hear from me every day that they make my heart happy. No matter what.

If you are a parent of older teens or young adults and you are feeling as though it's too late, it's not. I have had parents and children learn to joy-bond much later in life. Much healing and restoration can occur when you learn to create joy bonds.

Cindy's Story

My friend Cindy has an incredible story of relational restoration with her teenage son. She shares:

> *A few years ago, I was introduced to the concept of how a healthy balance of joy and quiet can change the brain. This was timely because my son, Max, had just begun his last year of high school and couldn't wait to leave home. I was afraid of losing him.*
>
> *When I learned that it's impossible for people to keep their brains from receiving joy and rest as long as the giver is truly happy to be with them, I decided I had nothing to*

lose. I knew it would really be a challenge since Max spent as little time at home as possible. In addition, I usually had a list of chores and other things I wanted to talk with him about, and these usually dominated any conversation we did have—much to his annoyance.

With my relational circuits turned on, I planted myself in the kitchen anytime I thought Max would be coming through the door and began practicing joy with him by a simple greeting. At first he wouldn't even look at me, so it all had to be done through tone of voice. After a few days of hearing my greeting with no request attached (my 'quiet'), he began to look in my direction. After many more days passed with still no request for chores or anything else, he began to occasionally linger for a few seconds. Eye contact followed, then words began to be exchanged.

I still refrained from making requests of him at this time (or doing any other sort of 'nagging'). I realized I had done so much damage by demanding things from him without putting our relationship first, and I wanted to make it clear I valued him more than any chore or other thing on my mind (like his grades). I found other ways to ask for what I needed outside of the few minutes of face-to-face interaction we had in the kitchen.

Months later when he left for college, things were improving but still quite tense. My husband and I weren't sure what would happen when he was off on his own. He was truly in God's hands. By God's grace, Max met some Christian guys and got involved in a freshman Bible study. By April, he invited us to his baptism and decided to spend his summer with this Bible study group, working a day job in a southern resort town and having spiritual and leadership training in the evenings and weekends.

Before Max left for that summer experience, I taught him Immanuel Journaling. Learning to hear God's voice and how to process his emotions with Immanuel introduced an entirely new level of transformation in his life. Over time, I also introduced him to others who are continuing to mentor him and help him find his footing to this day.

It's been nearly five years now, and Max and I have had many highs and lows along the way, but our trajectory continues in a positive direction. The relationship we have now—as hard as it still is at times—is far more valuable than any chore I thought would 'improve his character.' I now know that character change happens in healthy, joyful relationships full of peace and freedom. I'm so grateful to have learned these valuable insights because of the life and unspeakable joy and peace we enjoy now. In addition, the foundation of trust in our relationship is strengthening so that when misunderstandings and trials come our way, we are better able to keep our relationship above the problem.

Connection and the Nervous System

If identity is a house, secure attachment is the foundation. When attachment is done well, a person will feel secure in relationships. They will have a strong sense of belonging, hope, and optimism (Chapter 6). When our identity house is anchored deeply in a sense of belonging, we are secure. We know we will have ups and downs, but we are not alone.

Once a healthy foundation is laid, then we can begin building a structure. The walls and roof keep the good stuff in and the bad stuff out. Home should be where belonging happens, where we know that we are safe to be fully awake, alive, and free, and where we have people who are happy to be with us.

Healthy foundations form healthy wiring for connection and thriving. Think of the electrical wiring in a house as the nervous system. The system must be well grounded.

Deb Dana, in her book *The Polyvagal Theory in Therapy,* says, "Through the Social Engagement System, we use our eyes, our voice, and movement of our face and head to send and receive signals of safety and to reach out for and offer connection."[12] The social engagement system works on the fast track of our brain. The fast track works faster than conscious thought. Before we even know that we are happy to see someone, our brain has already responded.[13]

Imagine a little girl hearing the garage door go up. She knows that it is her daddy coming home from work. She jumps up from her game, yells, "Daddy's home" and runs for the back door. Her little brain is registering excitement and joy because all of her experience says that Daddy is always happy to see her. When that door opens, she's going to see Daddy's face light up. He is going to be happy to see her, and they will hug. These are joy bonds. They developed from years of in-

---

[12] Deb Dana, *The Polyvagal Theory in Therapy: Engaging the Rhythm of Regulation* (New York: W.W. Norton, 2018), 74.

[13] Marcus Warner and Jim Wilder, *Rare Leadership: 4 Uncommon Habits for Increasing Trust, Joy, and Engagement in the People You Lead* (Chicago: Moody, 2016).

teraction. She knows Daddy can have a bad day and even be grumpy, but he is always happy to see her.

Our brain continually looks for cues of safety or danger from the faces of those we are connected with. Our earliest experiences in this area will wire our system for either connection or protection. For our relational circuitry to engage well and wire us for connection, we need safe, joy-filled, face-to-face, eye-to-eye interactions.

Connection Disruptors

Many kinds of disruptions interfere with our connection wiring. When we experience fear while trying to attach instead of joy, our brains and nervous systems can wire for protection instead of connection. Parents who are chronically distracted or dysregulated can disrupt relational circuit wiring in their children. Chronic shame and trauma can disrupt connection. And of course, toxic relational styles can teach babies that connection is dangerous, resulting in fear bonds being created instead of joy bonds.

Fear bonds develop when a child knows they need their caregivers to survive, but those same caregivers also hurt them, scare them, or act unpredictably. Instead of that first little girl who heard the garage door go up, now picture another. She knows that it is her daddy. But her brain isn't wired to get excited. She starts to panic and feels fear. Some of her experience says that Daddy might be happy to see her, but he also might be really angry when he gets home. He might yell at her or, worse, not even see her at all. This little girl might run and hide behind a wall or piece of furniture until Daddy walks into the house. She may wait and observe first what mood Daddy is in. If she hears safety cues like a laugh or a happy tone in his voice, she may come out and sheepishly say, "Hi Dad!" If she hears danger cues like a frustrated tone or sees a certain facial expression, she may stay hidden until Daddy disappears into his room for the night. This is an example of a fear bond.

Distraction

One afternoon, I was standing in line at Target when I heard a sweet little "Hi" coming from behind me. I looked down to find a little girl, maybe two or three years old, sitting behind me in a sled. Her mother stood above her holding the rope at the other end of the sled they were waiting to purchase. I offered the little girl my eyes and a smile, and I answered, "Hi!" She paused, then asked, "Where's your phone?" The question seemed out of place until I looked around. I stood fourth in line for the register and the little girl's mother stood behind me. Every adult in line was looking down at their phones but me. I was the only person whose eyes were available. With another smile, I answered, "In my purse." Just then the mother looked up sheepishly, apologized for her daughter's curiosity, told the little girl to "shh," and then looked back at her phone.

My heart sank. How many times had I missed opportunities for connection and joy with my own children because I was distracted or hurried? I prayed a silent prayer of repentance and gratitude for the wake-up call, and then decided to plan a family game night for that evening.

We are becoming an increasingly distracted culture. I have often wondered what kind of impact this has had on our children's neurological development. Our children need to see our eyes and know that the smile on our face is because we are happy to be with them. Spending time together, making eye contact, laughing, and having fun is essential for healthy development.

Shame

Shame is one of the Big Six emotions that we will discuss in Chapter 4. But since shame is an attack on identity and identity is so closely related to attachments, we need to discuss the problem here in this context too.

Joy comes only through authentic relationships. We can't fake it. The brain can tell the difference. "Authentic" means that we are offering our true self to another to be seen for who we truly are. We cannot feel truly seen, known, and loved until others see the real us—including our weaknesses.

Our ability to connect is often linked to our nervous systems' assessment of safe or not safe. If our relationship experiences tell us that people are not safe, then our nervous systems will wire for survival (fear based) instead of connection (love based). The good news is that even if your nervous system has wired around fear, that wiring can be reshaped. You can move out of the protection patterns you learned from early relational experiences into patterns of connection. Your brain and body connections can rewire by experiencing the goodness of safe connection.

We all have a God-given need to be seen, known, and loved for who we truly are without the fear of rejection.[14] But because we live in a fallen world and are born dependent on broken people, we will each experience places in our story where we feel missed, rejected, and unseen. These experiences create shame.

Shame is a disconnector. When we feel shame, it cascades disconnecting effects through our whole being, disconnecting us from our own hearts, thoughts, feelings, and identities. It also sends signals to our true self to hide. Therefore, we feel disconnected from God and others.

Feeling shame is a part of the human experience. Learning to establish authentic connection and belonging are keys to bouncing back from shame.

---

14   Thompson, *Soul of Shame*, 124.

Authentic Connection Versus "Fitting In"

Brené Brown, in her book *Gifts of Imperfection,* defines the word *belonging* as "the innate human desire to be part of something larger than us." She says that "because this yearning is so primal, we often try to acquire it by fitting in and by seeking approval, which are not only hollow substitutes for belonging, but often barriers to it."[15] True belonging only happens when we present our authentic selves to the world.

Today, there is a mass assault on living out our authentic self, and as a result, on authentic relationship. Comparison, social media, "airbrushed" image building—these practices are leaving an entire generation feeling lonely, disconnected, and unseen (which is ironic since never before have we been so seen). We need to ask ourselves if what is being seen is our true authentic self or an airbrushed version of who we think the world wants us to be. Of course, trying to fit in is not the only way we respond to the world's assault on our authentic self. We can also live bitter and offended, rejecting and rebelling against what others value, or just plain hide ourselves away from the world hoping to stay off the radar.

Belonging is essential to the human experience. For us to feel that we belong, however, we must live out of our true selves. Fitting in is

---

15   Brené Brown, *The Gifts of Imperfection: Let Go of Who You Think You're Supposed to Be and Embrace Who You Are* (Center City: MN, Hazelden, 2010), 26.

about changing who we are to fit what we perceive the world wants us to be (false self). Fitting in leads to aloneness because genuine connection cannot happen if we hide our true self. Belonging is the opposite of fitting in. Belonging happens when we are who we were created to be and are able to connect with others who are being who they were created to be. Finding who we were created to be (our authentic self) requires us to connect with our heart.

A person experiencing relational shame will isolate, pull away from authentic connection, and find alternative forms of coping with pain. Since we were created for intimate relational connection and joy, when it's disrupted we feel attachment pain. Attachment pain is the worst kind of pain. This pain is what songs and movies are made of. Attachment pain is when we feel separated and disconnected from the ones we love.

Identifying Shame Messages

What does shame look like in our individual stories?

Shame forms something like a wall around our heart that keeps us disconnected. Shame says, "I don't fit in," "I don't belong here," "I'm not good enough," or "I'm too much." It says, "Nobody will ever love me the way I long to be loved. I don't measure up. Maybe if I _____, then will I be good enough?"

However, love says, "I love you always and forever no matter what." Love says, "You are my child. Nothing can separate you from my love. You don't have to earn my love; it's already there. You belong here just as you are. Just be you and rest in my arms." We all long for this kind of unconditional acceptance because we were created for it. When it gets disrupted, shame rushes in.

Shame often comes from places in our stories where our God-given longings and desires are unmet. At some point, we put ourselves out there longing to be seen, enjoyed, and valued, and it goes terribly wrong. If you have kids, you have heard "Watch me, Mommy" or "Watch me, Daddy"—this is the cry to be seen. Little girls ask, "Do you like my dress, Daddy?" as they give it a twirl, and young boys boast, "Look at my muscles, Momma!" as they flex their biceps. This is the cry of children to be delighted in and affirmed and told they are beautiful and strong.

When he came to my house, my nephew used to exclaim with a beaming smile, "It's me, I'm here!" You and I see these desires to be seen and valued as cute, don't we? But what happens if we were that child? What if we put ourself out there, risking our heart, but we were not received, delighted in, and cherished? What if we didn't receive the connection and affirmation we wanted and needed? As children, we are excellent observers but terrible interpreters. We don't see those discrepancies as a product of the fall of humanity or our parents' own brokenness, but instead we interpret our experiences to mean that something must be wrong with us.

Where were you left feeling disappointed, hurt, humiliated, foolish, dirty, stupid, or unwanted? Shame messages really aren't hard to find. They are in the words that scroll across our minds a thousand times a day. The problem is that they are so much a part of us that we often don't notice them. They are our normal.

Beth's Story

Beth's story is an everyday example of how shame can enter into the life of a child:

> *In my house growing up, order and keeping a clean house were top priorities. Both of my parents could be described as "type A" and "perfectionistic." I think it would be helpful here to understand my personality. If type A is one end of a personality spectrum, I would be at the far other end. I was very dramatic, creative, full of expression, free spirited, and strong willed. The skills necessary for picking up my room were just not there yet. When my mom or dad spoke the words, "Go clean your room," I remember the flooding feeling that would overtake me. I would feel overwhelmed and think, "What is wrong with me that I can't do this 'easy thing?'"*
>
> *I remember one day my mom told me to go clean my room because it was a mess. When she returned about an hour later, she found the room even messier than it was before, because of course, I got caught up in my imagination and started to play instead of clean. At this point, something triggered in my mom. She flooded with her own emotions and flew into*

a rage. She acted out her anger in ways that she would later regret and apologize for. Then I watched as the guilt she felt over her rage sent her into a dark place of despair. In those moments, I made profound agreements with the enemy about who I was.

I can still see the look on my mom's face and feel the warmth of shame in my checks. After my mom left, I sat alone in my room in front of a very messy closet. I decided that something was horribly wrong with me. This is where the enemy of our soul likes to rush in and whisper lies. In those moments, I made agreements with the enemy that I was no good, messy, dangerous, and defective. I was capable of sending my most cherished person in the world into dark places of despair. My mom acted out of her brokenness (as we all do), the enemy used it, and I bought the lies.

This story highlights the difference between guilt and shame. Beth was not feeling guilty because she disobeyed her mom; she was feeling shame because she believed in that moment that she was something wrong and defective. This was an attack on identity. The enemy is opportunistic. He uses our times of pain to introduce lies. He wants us to believe who he says we are, not who God says we are.

This incident stayed buried in Beth's heart for many years. Whenever she felt that she didn't measure up, that she was messy, or that she had disappointed someone, she would spiral into a deep place of shame and re-agree with the enemy's lies. Many years later, however, Beth invited Jesus into this wound. When Beth saw that Jesus was with her and that he delighted in her messy, curly hair and carefree heart, the truth of the look on his face replaced the pain of her traumatic memory. Jesus brought the truth of his love and healing presence into the wound, healing it forever.

This is an example of returning to joy (attachment and connection) from shame. In this example, connection with Jesus was powerful to bring healing. This is also an example of repairing a hole in the capacity bubble after a flat. For more information on emotional healing and fixing flats see Marcus Warner's book, *Understanding the Wounded Heart,* or his e-course on emotional healing.

Connection Makers

Identity is formed in the context of relationship. So when we have no joy bonds fueling our brain, identity gets disrupted. Shame rushes into the places where joy should be, we feel attachment pain, and because we are meaning-making machines, we write stories in our heads about why we are unlovable or unacceptable. We believe lies about who we are. Thankfully the story keeps going. Jesus modeled something for us that works as a bridge from shame and disconnection to connection and joy—he modeled vulnerability.

When we allow ourselves to be vulnerable and connect with God, our own authentic hearts, and others, we form a three-strand rope that anchors us during the storms of life. This anchor builds hope and our capacity to do hard things. As followers of Jesus, we are firmly rooted in God's love. God's love, *agape* in Greek and *ḥesed* in Hebrew, is covenant love, like an "I will love you always and forever no matter what" kind of love.

We discussed earlier the beautiful joy-bonding that happens between a baby and parents as they make eye contact and play games like peek-a-boo. This creates the kind of bond that says, "You can throw-up on me, poop on me, and wake me up at all hours of the night, but I will still think that you are the most amazing little human ever!" This is the love that our heavenly Father feels for us. It is covenant love that guarantees we will never be alone, we belong to the King of Kings, and we are loved with an everlasting love. Hebrews 6:19–20 says, "We have this hope as an anchor for the soul, firm and secure. It enters the inner sanctuary behind the curtain, where our forerunner, Jesus, has entered on our behalf." This passage says to us that we get to be with the God of the universe in the Holy of Holies, the most intimate place. Unfortunately, many of us have never known this kind of love; consequently, we can't imagine God feeling this way about us.

Connection through Conflict: Returning from Shame

Shame resilience refers to our ability to reconnect after being triggered in shame. We will all experience shame in relationship, but how do we come back from it? Shame disconnects us from others and our own heart. Learning to reconnect after being triggered in shame is essential. We can learn relational skills such as being able to stay connected in conflict, making the relationship bigger than the conflict, and speaking truth in loving ways. Resolving conflict and restoring connection are essential to creating belonging.

I remember the first time that I felt as though I had really messed up in my marriage. I was so scared that my husband would decide he had made a mistake marrying me. My shame messages were screaming loudly in my head. My instinct in shame was to run and hide and make up a version of the narrative that blamed him for the problem. Those reactions are exactly how Adam and Eve handled their shame. But instead, I prayed. I asked Jesus for help. I remembered that Jesus loves me always and forever no matter what. This gave me the strength to apologize to my husband. I owned my mistake. I was blown away by his response. He said, "No big deal. It's OK, I love you. This is marriage. We will make mistakes, hurt each other, talk it through, and be OK."

I believed that if I made too big a mistake it would change his love for me. I was afraid that he would never see me the same way again. I held deeply rooted shame messages about messing up, but my husband saw it very differently. He was much better at making mistakes than I was. His ability to stay relational during our conflict demolished the shame messages I was believing and wrote truth in their place, which healed my heart and made our bond even stronger. I had never felt so loved. My husband taught me that conflict plus resolution equals greater intimacy.

Because we become wounded in the context of relationship, healing also happens in the context of relationship. When our foundation is laid with a dysfunctional pattern of relating, the old pattern must be disrupted; we must have new experiences of relating that surprise us and set new expectations.

A Word about Addictions

We are beginning to see an increase in addiction among our youth. Our brains are designed to run on joy and true relational joy cannot be counterfeited. If someone has no access to true relational joy, they will begin turning to dopamine to feel happy. Likes on social media, drugs, alcohol, adrenaline, sexual exploration, pornography, and eating disorders can all produce the chemical "dopamine" in the brain and can become either joy substitutes or an attempt to numb the pain from a lack of true joy. Now more than ever our children need us to engage with them, walk with them, and attune to their hearts. They are navigating a very rocky terrain.

Identity-Building Activities

Group Activity: Read *The Amazing Marvelous Milly* by Stefanie Hinman. Discuss God's love. Name as many things as you can from

God's word that tells us who God says we are. Discuss how to hear God's voice speaking into our lives. Practice hearing from him.

Reflection questions: What lies have you believed? What does God say about you? What do you believe about God? Is he trustworthy?

***

Art Directive: What does shame look like? Have each participant draw and write about a time they felt shame. What were the lies they believed? In discussion, normalize the experience of shame. We all feel shame. Our stories may be different, but shame always feels like shame. We want to run, hide, cover, and blame.

***

Art Directive: What's true about me? Have each participant write the truth from God's word and practice listening for God's voice. Who does he say that you are? Make something new with the truth.

***

Art Directive: Treasure box. Each participant has an opportunity to paint and decorate a small treasure box or shoe box with affirmations about who they are. Inside the box the participant can write or symbolize the things that are at the core of who they are. These are the things that they share only with safe and trusted people. On the outside of the box the participant can depict the aspects of themselves that they share with most people.

Tools for Building Relational Connection

Gratitude

It can be hard to retrain the brain for gratitude. I look at gratitude as a muscle that needs to be built. At first it can feel forced to look for things to be thankful for or appreciate because many of us have brains trained to find threats, not beauty—especially those of us who have endured trauma or a lot of adversity. The amygdala becomes overactive, always perceiving danger. This state is often referred to as "hypervigilant." Thoughts race as we always create worst-case scenarios in our heads. If you relate to this kind of functioning yourself or see it in your child, I have good news: you can retrain the brain to pick up on the safety cues that are all around you and move the brain from danger mode to safety mode.

Recently I bought a new minivan. I really liked the color. On the way home from the dealer, however, I began to notice many vans in the same color on the road. Then coming out of the grocery store one day and looking for my van, I noticed that every other car in the lot looked like mine. I had bought the most popular van model and color in the world. I never noticed this trend before because my brain wasn't trained to see it. Now I was seeing vans like mine everywhere I went. What we pay attention to affects our perspective.

Learning to orient toward gratitude and learning to recognize our connections are powerful tools for retraining the brain and body for SCC (safe, calm, and connected). These tools send signals to the nervous system that says we are safe and can rest. The more you practice them, the stronger your gratitude muscle grows. We will discuss further how this process works when we discuss the concept of story.

Gratitude Activities

Activity: Identify what fills your capacity bubble. Identify when your air is low. Learn skills for replenishment.

Appreciation hunt: Begin making a list of things that you love and bring you joy. Go out with your phone or your camera and start taking pictures of those things (for example: sunrises, sunsets, flowers, family fun, laughter). Document these times, draw about them, journal about them. Begin to grow your appreciation muscle. At the dinner table, name three things you appreciated from the day.

***

Family gratitude jar: On the topic of gratitude and remembrance, most things that bring us joy do so because they remind us of a time we felt safe, calm, and connected. You can build a Rolodex of "joy bombs" by remembering times that brought you joy. Have you ever been driving down the road and a song comes on and immediately you are flooded with joy? Your foot starts tapping and you start singing because you love this song! You might stop and ask, "Why do I love this song?" Maybe a happy memory is attached. When you have an experience like this, write it down. If you are walking along a trail and see a beautiful flower, take a picture. Pay attention to the beautiful things around you. Even on rainy days we can find beauty. Write these experiences on slips of paper or print small photos and save them in a jar. This practice begins to teach our brain to look for things to be thankful for.

***

Family project: gratitude album. Make a family gratitude photo album. Everyone takes pictures of things they enjoy and are thankful for.

Connected and Safe Activities

Discussion: Define *resilience*. Ask the children if they have ever heard this word. What do they think it might mean? We can't always control or change our situations or what happens to us, but we can choose how we respond. When the hard stuff happens, we can learn to bend without breaking. We become more resilient as we build emotional capacity.

***

Activity: Bending but not breaking. Pass out pipe cleaners (or any flexible object like a paper clip or small wire) and have the children bend their pipe cleaners into various shapes. While working on this activity, talk about how the pipe cleaners bend but don't break. They can be molded, bent, and changed in shape, but they don't break.

***

Art Directive: Helping hand. *(Materials include paper and pencils, colored pencils, markers, or crayons)* What does connected and safe feel like? Have the child trace the outline of their hand on a piece of paper. Then have them write their own name in the palm of the hand, and write the names of the people who support them on each finger. Discuss the importance of the people who love them and who are there to help them when they have needs. This activity helps identify supportive people in the child's life.

***

Connection and trust building activities: Eye contact with others helps to make beautiful neurological connections in the brain. Playing games that incorporate eye contact will help to create connection and safety in the group.

Keep in mind that too much eye contact can be overwhelming. We must build rest into the game as well. Play one game, then rest and do something quiet that doesn't involve eye contact, like coloring or reading a book. Joy and rest are two sides of the same coin. They build together. We will discuss rest more in the next chapter.

***

Hand slap game with eye contact: Two players stand facing each other with their hands out. Player 1 goes first, placing their hands under player 2's hands. Player 1 tries to dart their hands out from under player 2's hands to slap the top of player 2's hands. The players are to maintain eye contact throughout the game. The game tests reflexes and quickness of hands. When player 1 is successful at slapping player 2's hands, the players switch places.

***

Staring contest: In this game, player 1 and player 2 stare at each other without blinking for as long as they can. Whoever goes the longest without blinking wins.

***

Football straws with eye contact: In this game, you will need straws and cotton balls. The group members will pair up, each with a straw in their mouth. They blow on a single cotton ball to try to move the cotton ball into the other person's goal.

***

Mirroring games: Mirroring is a very powerful way to build neuropathways in the brain. You can make it a game by playing "Follow the Leader" or "Simon Says." Walk on your toes, walk on your heels, walk backward, and then bump into each other, laugh, and fall down. When that feels comfortable, you can face each other, making eye contact, and mirror big arm movements and dance moves. Keep it light and fun.

***

Mirroring as an attunement exercise: *(Works best with family members)* One family member stands directly in front of another. They take turns being the mirror. This means that they copy exactly what the other is doing at the same time they are doing it. This means that the second participant (mirror) must anticipate what the first participant (mover) is about to do. Start moving very slowly so that the mirror has a chance to think about where and how the first participant will be moving.

Chapter Four

Bouncing Back: Navigate Emotions

Triggers cause us to feel overwhelmed. They are different for everyone—what triggers me is different from what triggers you. But what happens in the body is the same for everyone: the ANS (autonomic nervous system) switch gets flipped and stress hormones flood in, affecting how we perceive the event. We can go from calm to overwhelmed immediately, like flipping on a light switch, but it takes time to go from overwhelmed to calm (like turning a dimmer switch). Yet we can learn ways to help our body return to calm.

Dan is a seventeen-year-old high school student. He has a short fuse. When he feels challenged in any way, he flips his lid and he explodes with anger. When in a rage, Dan loses control over his behavior. This has led to him being kicked out of several schools. Dan knows that if he explodes one more time he will not be allowed to graduate with his class. He also believes that he has no ability to control his temper and fears that if someone looks at him the wrong way, he might fight again.

Thankfully, the new school counselor understands the neurobiology of trauma. She began working with Dan to help him recognize his triggers and to identify the first signs that he is getting triggered so that he can work on his calming strategies before he loses control of his temper. Dan is also learning to connect his fight instinct to survival needs that were unmet when he was a young boy, and he is learning new ways to get those needs met.

After several weeks of working with the school counselor, Dan proudly stopped by her office one day after school and announced, "I did it! My teacher pissed me off, but I felt my jaw start to tighten and my body tense up, and instead of losing control I did my calm down exercise. I didn't explode!" Dan was beginning to feel empowered to choose his own behavior.

Returning to Joy from Overwhelming Emotions

The very term *bouncing back* indicates that there is something positive to return to. In Chapter 3, we discussed creating an internal sense of "home base" for our children so that they have a firm foundation from which to explore life. This chapter will discuss building pathways for returning home from life's big adventures. We must learn how to venture out into our world, experience all that it has to offer, and then find our way back home to rest, reconnect, and recover.

In this chapter, we will discuss the first three of five skills for bouncing back. These skills teach us to navigate our emotions:

>**Skill #1. Identify emotions.** Recognize what emotions feel like in the body and learn to distinguish between emotions.
>
>**Skill #2. Name and normalize emotions.** Integrate the emotional/feeling brain and the thinking/rational brain by giving the feeling a name and accepting that emotions are a normal part of the human experience.
>
>**Skill #3. Express emotions.** Assign meaning and story to feelings and express them in healthy and appropriate ways.

We will explore the full range of human emotions, healthy emotional expressiveness, and the Big Six overwhelming emotions, including how to find our way back home from them.

In the next chapter, we will discuss skills #4 and #5 ("Return to calm" and "Refill") and ways to bring awareness to our unconscious system of assessing safety.

Our Rainbow of Emotions

Emotions are like breathing. We all have them; they are a part of being alive. Just as we take a deep breath, use the oxygen to fuel our body, and then exhale the carbon dioxide, we can learn to feel our feelings, be curious about them, and then release them. We can learn from the experience of our emotions and then return to SCC (safe, calm, and connected).

Just like colors of the rainbow, we all have a range of emotions. Some may feel better than others, but each adds color to our days. It would be boring to live in a world without color. Emotions bring animation and beauty to our world. They become a problem only when they become overwhelming. We feel overwhelmed when we perceive that we lack the internal or external resources to come back from them.

The science of interpersonal neurobiology tells us that our brains must build pathways back to SCC from overwhelming emotions. When an individual does not have a fully functioning joy center or pathways back from overwhelming emotions, they tend to get stuck in unhealthy survival patterns such as fear and anxiety, dissociation, and numbing by turning to drugs and alcohol.

According to Wilder and Warner in *Rare Leadership*, six big emotions tend to be the most overwhelming. The "Big Six" are shame, anger, disgust, sadness, fear, and hopeless despair.[16] I also like to recognize that grief and attachment pain are among the most overwhelming complex emotions because they are a combination of any of these six emotions in the context of loss. Just as I needed to find my way home from the grocery store, church, school, and the gas station after we moved, we need to learn our way home from each of the Bix Six.

For years I facilitated support groups for children who either had a chronically ill parent, were anticipating losing a parent due to illness, or had lost a parent. We spent much of the time discussing healthy emotional expressiveness. Without fail, one or two kids in the group

---

16   Warner and Wilder, *Rare Leadership*, 161–168.

would start to feel overwhelming emotions during the discussion but did not have the skills to express what they were feeling. They would begin to disrupt the group, change the subject, or attempt to derail the conversation. We recognized the reasons for the disruptive behavior and were able to help the children find words or pictures to name and express what they were feeling. The group was able to provide a safe place for empathy and connection. We saw many children flourish as they gained the skills to express themselves, be heard and seen, and find comfort in not being alone.

Helping Children Navigate Feelings

Feelings are tools. They serve a purpose. They give us information. You can think of them as warning lights on a dashboard. They don't define what is true, they only give us information. We need to learn to pay attention to feelings in ourselves and others and to be curious about why they are present. If the "check engine" light comes on, it means the car has a problem. But until you look under the hood, you cannot know if the problem is big or minor.

We can also think of emotions like the waves of the ocean. Some are small and some are big. Some waves knock us down when they come in, as do some emotions. An important part of learning to stand back up is naming our emotions accurately so that we give them context and meaning.

Two common, unhealthy ways of coping with uncomfortable emotions are stuffing them or exploding. Stuffing, ignoring, or locking down feelings is like holding a beach ball under the water. We cannot hold the ball down forever. It will eventually pop back up. Exploding feelings are like opening a soda can too fast after it has been shaken or letting go of an untied balloon after blowing it full of air and watching it fly around the room. It is better to acknowledge what we are feeling by naming the emotion (or emotions) accurately. Then we can release the energy from our feelings slowly and calmly.

The Process of Emotional Expressiveness

The first skill in learning healthy emotional expressiveness is learning to differentiate between feelings. The second and third skills are naming emotions and making meaning from them. While each skill is a separate developmental task, they can all be learned at the same time.

We learn to identify what each feeling feels like in the body, recognize the expressions they make on our faces, and give the feelings a name. We then make meaning of our experiences in the form of a story that can be told. These tasks engage the left and right hemispheres of the brain, integrating the experience into a whole, and are often performed naturally as parents and children do life together. You can make it a game, however, by making funny feeling faces in a mirror. Name the different feelings and make the faces together. Then discuss what each feeling feels like in the body and normalize it as a natural part of being alive. We do not have to be afraid of our feelings, but we can learn from them.

When a child is able to integrate words and feelings, this allows them to then assign meaning to the experience. Assigning meaning helps put the experience into a story that can be told. Telling a story is how the experience is able to be expressed so that a person is able to return to SCC and then refill their capacity bubble (skills #4 and #5).

Children often need the help of an adult to first identify and name what they are feeling (skills #1 and #2) and then to assign meaning to experiences (skill #3). If left on their own to navigate their emotional world, children will most likely adopt unhealthy belief systems. When a child has an attuned adult to help them process pain, overwhelming experiences are integrated and resolved. I consider this process "trauma mitigation," and it's a beautiful gift to give your child. More on using story in Chapter 6.

Nonverbal Expression

Before a child can use words to describe overwhelming, big emotions, they will first express themselves through behavior. Help them express their feelings in appropriate, nonverbal ways. Here are some options:
- ☐ deep breathing
- ☐ jumping jacks
- ☐ running in place
- ☐ jump rope
- ☐ crying
- ☐ scribbling really hard with a crayon on paper
- ☐ drawing a picture about how their heart feels
- ☐ playdough
- ☐ squeezing a stress ball—or any activity that engages the senses

Artistic expression also helps children nonverbally voice what they are feeling. Creative expression comes naturally for children. Spend time with any child and you will see creativity at work through imagination, dance, song, story, and art. Creative expression combined with "story work" (Chapter 6) engages both the left and the right sides of the brain. This helps a child fully process and integrate their experiences, both positive and negative. Creative expression also provides a nonthreatening way to communicate with children, bypassing many of the defenses and developmental deficiencies that make traditional talk therapy challenging. Talk therapy is even harder when children have had trauma.

After a child has calmed down, help them name their feelings and tell their story. This helps them to return to feeling safe and connected.

Feeling Activities: Skills #1 & #2

Feelings face cards *(works well for younger kids):* You can purchase face cards, or you can pre-cut faces demonstrating a variety of emotions and representing a variety of cultures. The facilitator holds up each card and asks the children to identify its feeling. Choosing one card/feeling, the child draws a picture of that emotion.

***

Mirror game *(works well for younger kids):* Provide a handheld mirror for each child. Have them practice naming and making feeling faces in the mirror.

***

Art Directive: How my heart feels *(Materials include paper and pencils, colored pencils, markers, play dough, or crayons):* Discuss how feelings are like the colors of the rainbow. Each person gets to name what feeling is represented by each color. The children can write inscriptions identifying which feeling names they assigned to each color. Discuss how we can feel more than one feeling at a time. Have each child name what feeling they are having in the current moment. They can then color a heart with the colors that match what they are feeling. They can color light or dark depending on the intensity of the feeling. Example: If sad=blue, they might color half of the heart in blue. If using play dough, each child can take the amount of play dough to represent the amount of the feeling they are currently feeling.

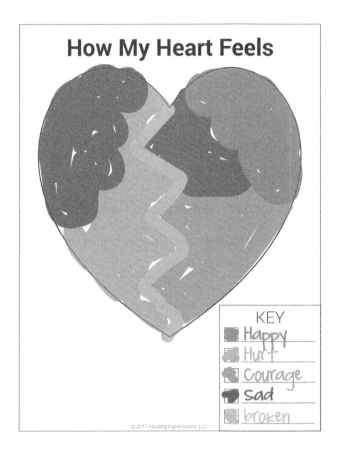

(See program manual for colored diagrams)

***

Discussion: Feeling questions. Discuss the following list of questions.

1. Name as many feelings as you can.
2. What does a _____ face look like? *(everyone makes the face)*
3. What kinds of things make a person feel _____?
4. What feeling word would you associate with each color _____?

5. Can you identify where you feel that in your body?
6. Do our feelings change who we are?

• •

Art Directive: Feeling rainbow. *(Materials include paper and pencils, colored pencils, markers, and crayons OR paint [red, blue, yellow, white and black], paint brushes, and paper plates.)* This directive can range from very simple to more complex *(see extended version, listed next)*. In the simple version, you discuss the colors of the rainbow and feelings as all being on a spectrum. You can have the children come up with as many different feelings as they can. Then draw or paint a rainbow on which the child organizes their feelings and assigns each feeling a color.

• •

Art Directive: Primary vs. secondary emotions. *(Materials for the extended version include a paint pallet, the three primary paint colors [red, yellow, blue], and also white and black paint.)* Have the children place the three primary colors in a triangle on their paint pallets and mix the primary colors to create secondary colors *(see illustration that follows)*. Discuss how primary colors must be found in nature—you cannot mix them. However, secondary emotions can be created by mixing primary colors together. Have the children mix two primary colors together to create a third completely new color. Discuss how some feelings like anger are actually secondary feelings because they always have other feelings (like hurt, shame, or fear) underneath them. Mix each color with white and black and discuss the intensity of emotions. (*To lighten a color, start with white and add the color to it to gradually increase the intensity. To darken a color, you will want to start with the color and gradually add black to it to darken it.*)

(See program manual for colored diagrams)

Follow-up discussion: Describe the full range of human emotions, explaining how all people have a full range of emotions including the ones that feel good, the ones that feel bad, and the ones that feel ugly. We can't pick and choose what feelings we have just as we can't pick the weather. We will experience them all as humans. Discuss what a spectrum is using the example of a rainbow. Show how colors vary from light to dark. You can pick a feeling such as anger and show how many variations of the emotion the group can come up with (examples: irritated, frustrated, grumpy, mad, angry, furious, irate).

Next, the children can share their pictures, talking about how they labeled the feelings. Discuss how feelings that do not feel "good" can still serve a good purpose, like lights on a dashboard. Once we identify the purpose of a feeling, we can release it again. This is called "feeling fishing." We catch the feeling and then release it back. A metaphor of fishing can be helpful in teaching kids to identify their feelings, ask the important questions, and then let go of them. We do not need to judge our feelings, only be curious about why we are feeling them.

A good way to illustrate this is discussing the differences between physical and emotional pain. When we touch a hot stove, it may really hurt. However, the pain serves a purpose. It is meant to send a signal from the brain to the body so we quickly remove our hand from the stove to keep a really bad burn from happening. What is true with physical pain is also true with emotional pain. Our pain teaches us.

***

Art Directive: Inside/outside mask. *(Materials include paper and pencils, colored pencils, markers, or crayons. Papier-mâché is optional.)* A mask is a helpful tool for teaching kids about the metaphorical masks we often wear over our hearts. Discuss the times when what we're feeling on the outside doesn't match what we're feeling on the inside. The children can use a paper plate, hole-punched and tied with string, or they can actually make masks out of papier-mâché. On the inside of the mask, have the children write or draw things about themselves that not everyone knows—thoughts, feelings, and facts that they share with their most trusted relationships. On the outside of the mask, have them write or draw thoughts, feelings, and facts about themselves that are common knowledge. This is a good opportunity to talk about being our true self, earning trust, and choosing who we share our heart with carefully.

Expressing Emotion in Healthy Ways Activities:

Skill #3

Talking about high energy emotions like anger and fear

Discussion: Explain how (as mentioned previously) there are two common, unhealthy ways of coping with uncomfortable emotions: stuffing and/or exploding. Stuffing, or locking down feelings, is like holding a beach ball down under the water. It will eventually pop back up. Exploding feelings are like opening a pop can too fast after it has been shaken or letting go of a balloon full of air and watching it fly around the room. It is better to release the feelings slowly and calmly. This can be done by assigning names to feelings so that they can be felt, learned from, and released. Feeling emotions without naming them is, like Brené Brown says, "swimming with one arm." Naming emotions without feeling them requires us to disconnect from our heart and this disconnects us from joy. We cannot pick and choose what feeling we want. We must feel them all. If we try to disconnect from them, we will lose the ones that feel good too.

***

Demonstration: *Step 1.* Pass a soda bottle around the room and ask each participant to give it a good shake. Stop and ask who wants to open it up. Releasing high energy emotions like anger works like releasing pressure from a soda bottle. You open it just a little, then close it back up, then open it again just a little, then close it back up. The trick to releasing stronger emotions, like anger, is to release them slowly over time. (It also works well to bring two soda bottles into the room for the demonstration. Shake both. Open one and watch it explode, then open the other as described above.)

Step 2. Have the child think of something that made them mad recently. Ask, "Where do you feel anger in your body?"

- ☐ Invite them to practice releasing this high energy emotion from the body by balling up their fists, squeezing the muscles in their body all at once, then slowly relaxing their grip and wiggling their fingers.
- ☐ Encourage them to notice where the tension is in their body and begin relaxing each muscle group where they feel tension, one at a time. Check in with each muscle group from head to toe.
- ☐ When all the muscles have been relaxed, shake it all out.

Have the kids stand up and shake their limbs and body as if doing the hokey-pokey.

☐ Start the squeeze, release, and relax process all over again. Notice when the tension has released and the body feels calm. The goal is to bring awareness to when the emotion is present so it can be acknowledged and the high-stimulation energy can be released slowly and safely.

Creating Safe Spaces to Help Others Return to SCC

When our children are flooded with intense emotions, they may start to act out what they are feeling. At this point it's tempting to discipline our child for bad behavior. Instead, we can practice attunement. Attunement requires us to connect by meeting children in their big emotions. Comfort them by loaning them your PFC (prefrontal cortex) and regulated nervous system and help them return to a state of SCC.

Provide a Safe Place to Connect

Provide a safe space for people to feel their feelings and share them without being shut down or minimized. You can validate a person's emotion without agreeing with their narrative. Help them name what they are feeling if they cannot. A person can usually tell you if you have named it correctly.

Respond with Empathy

You might say something like, "It really hurts to feel disrespected—that makes sense to me. I wonder if you felt misunderstood?"

With young children, use simpler terms: "Are you feeling angry? I can see from your face that you look angry. Mommy gets angry too sometimes."

Comfort and Calm

Provide co-regulation with your presence. By sitting with them in their big emotions, you are communicating, "You are not alone. God is with us in our big emotions, and I am with you in your big emotions. I can sit with you in these emotions; they are not too much for me. I can loan you my regulated nervous system and emotional capacity so the problem doesn't feel quite so big."

With young children, you might say, "Let's do ten jumping jacks and take some really big breaths." After the child is calm, ask, "Can you tell me why you feel angry?" If the child is able to explain, "I'm mad because Tommy stole my bear," the caregiver can validate how frustrating it can be when someone takes our stuff and offer healthier ways of expressing the frustration.

Recover and Grow

Once the child has returned to calm and feels seen, heard, and attuned with, it can be a good time to offer discipline, advice, encouragement, a new perspective, truth from God's Word, or your own experience dealing with an issue. Sometimes a child will just need time to calm down. Going for a walk, bike ride, or doing something physical can help to burn off the stress hormones caused by the big emotion.

The more often this process happens, the more emotional resilience the child will develop. A child will need to go through this process with every big emotion multiple times to build strong pathways back to joy. Once these pathways become well developed, the child can begin to soothe themselves as they learn to regulate on their own.

Learning to respond well to children who are feeling big emotions is challenging. Let's take a deeper dive into how to respond well.

Responding Well to Older Kids, Children with Difficult Stories, and/or Other Adults

(Adapted from the teaching of Open Heart Ministries)

How we respond to people when they share their heart with us will greatly affect whether the interaction is healing or harmful. When people share their deeper feelings for the first time, they are like a turtle peeking out of its shell. If responses are empathetic and comforting, the turtle will come out further and share a little more. If the responses are dismissive, shaming, or harsh, they may not risk sharing again. As caregivers, we want to learn how to respond to the hearts of our children with empathy. This teaches them that they can come to us when they are struggling.

It is so important that our children know they are free to be their true selves and express their real feelings with us. We can be super tempted to correct or shame our children for the behavior they are exhibiting, but it's important that we learn to see behind the behavior and into their hearts. This way we are not just correcting the behavior but the belief or issue fueling the behavior.

A Response That Validates

We can validate people and communicate that they are valuable and their needs matter without saying that their behavior is acceptable.

Dr. Brené Brown says:

> If you put shame in a petri dish, it needs three ingre-

dients to grow exponentially: secrecy, silence, and judgment. If you put the same amount of shame in the petri dish and douse it with empathy, it can't survive.[17]

Whenever people open up and share an emotion, there is a moment of shame. They wonder if they have driven you away or made you regret listening. Here are two thoughts that can help you become an empathetic listener:

- Every time someone shares with you from his or her heart, receive it as a gift. Hold it gently.
- It is not the response itself that makes the difference. It is the connection created that brings comfort and healing.

Responses that Invalidate

It's also helpful to know which responses to avoid. Here are a few to keep in mind.

Self-focus: Avoid making the conversation *about you* when someone has opened up about their problems and their emotions. There is a place for telling your own story but not until you have been empathetic and validated the sharer first. The response, "Me too," is very powerful, but going into details about your own story shifts the focus away from the person who just shared and can leave him or her feeling exposed.

Wait until the person has both finished sharing and received an

---

17   Brené Brown, "Listening to Shame," filmed in New York March 2012, https://www.youtube.com/watch?v=psN1DORYYV0.

empathic, kind response before sharing your "me too" story. You can say something like, "I can relate." Saying "I know exactly how you feel" isn't helpful, however, because no two stories are exactly the same. It is better to say, "I can imagine how that would feel. It sounds painful," or "I can relate to feeling rejected. I have experienced rejection and it's really painful."

Subject-changing: Avoid remaining quiet or changing the subject. These are just ways of avoiding difficult emotions. If you find yourself doing that, it can be helpful to ask yourself, "What am I trying to avoid?"

Sharing advice too soon: Avoid giving advice or teaching until the proper time. There is a time and a place for teaching and giving advice, but in these sacred moments when a person has been vulnerable and shared their feelings, teaching and advice can feel shaming. The person can feel as though there is something wrong with what they shared. It can trigger thoughts like, "I'm so stupid for feeling this way or acting this way. Everyone is smarter than me." This also shifts the focus away from the person sharing and onto the advice giver.

Simplistic answers: Avoid minimizing or giving easy answers. If someone tells you they struggle with anxiety, don't say, "You know fear is a sin. We are commanded not to be afraid over three hundred times in the Bible." That is not helpful. Besides, the command not to be afraid is meant as an encouragement not a condemnation.

What Happens If Someone's Story Triggers Emotion in You?

Our natural response to vulnerability is often to rush in and rescue. We try to fix or shut down the emotions we hear instead of meeting them in those emotions. Empathy is the best response to vulnerability. Sitting with people in their tears and validating what they have been through can be painful, but it's worth it. It's the essence of compassion, which literally means "to share pain." Here are some suggestions for handling emotions you feel when listening to someone else's story:

1. Notice how you are responding to their story.
2. If you start to feel overwhelmed by your own emotions, take a few deep breaths. It's OK for them to see your tears; it lets them know you care.
3. If you know that you responded poorly at some point, just apologize. Conflict + Reconciliation = Connection.

We don't want to shut down or rescue a heart that is expressing pain. When someone starts to cry and express pain, it can trigger our own emotions and we may find ourselves trying to shut down their emotions, stop their crying, or distract them from their heart-felt emotions by giving an easy answer, or offering a quick solution before the pain has had a chance to come up and out. We may also try to rescue them by taking their problems on ourselves and making them ours to fix. This is a codependent response and isn't helpful. Pain and grief need to be expressed before they can be released, not pushed back down to fester. Rescuing a person from their pain sends the message that they are powerless and keeps them stuck in a victim mentality. Neither of these outcomes are helpful.

What we can do is enter into this sacred space with the person and let them know they are not alone.

Reminders for Responding to Vulnerability

- ☐ Speak in a calm, even voice.
- ☐ Use their name.
- ☐ Make eye contact.
- ☐ Use open body language. Don't cross your arms or put your hands in your pockets.
- ☐ Keep conversations and questions simple. It's not a good time to teach others when they are stuck in shame. Shame shuts down the learning centers. Instead, we need to serve them and meet their needs.

Practicing Empathy

Empathy provides **space for people to feel their own feelings and connect their own dots.** It sends the message that they can do this. Rescuing people sends the message, "I don't think you can handle this," and adds shame to the big emotions they already feel. If you often find yourself shutting others down or rescuing them, you may want to get curious about that. It may be an attempt to cope with your own unresolved heart issues.

There are only two essential ingredients to an empathetic response: **be authentic and be kind.** Good, empathetic responses handle shame gently. Empathy gives verbal hugs to people in pain. We do this by listening for shame statements and the places of pain in people's stories and connecting kindly and authentically in those places. Grace-filled words are powerful for creating connection.

1. **Share authentic emotion.** Empathy takes content from someone's story and feels something from that story with the person. For example, you might say, "I can understand why you reacted that way. It makes me mad, too, that your brother would do those things to you, and then tell you to keep it quiet." This is entering into their pain with them in a way that communicates, "My heart has connected with what you just shared."

2. **Highlight dignity.** Empathy speaks to the dignity it sees in people.
   - ☐ "I see such beauty in you."
   - ☐ "It was so brave of you to finally leave."
   - ☐ "I admire your strength."
   - ☐ "I admire your resilience."

3. **Observe virtue**. Empathy responds to statements of shame

with observations of virtue. Some examples of this include:

- Hearing: "I was so stupid."
    1. Responding: "I see you to be a smart little girl... You stood up and said no."
- Hearing: "I was such a coward."
    2. Responding: "I find you to be a brave and courageous young man. Thank you for sharing."
- Hearing: "I can't believe I went back."
    3. Responding: "It makes sense to me that you went back. He was your dad. He should have been your protector."

Chapter Five

Bouncing Back: Calm and Refill

In Chapter 4, we discussed helping children become more aware of their feelings and learn to express them in healthy ways. In this chapter, we will look at the wiring that can keep us in or near a triggered state and learn how to address those triggers so that we can return more easily to SCC (safe, calm, and connected). We will also consider ways to refill the air in our ball when it gets low so that we can maintain better bounce and stay resilient.

Here are the final two skills of the five needed for bouncing back. These skills help us calm and refill.

Skill #4. Return to SCC. Regulate our nervous system and gain awareness of what our unconscious system labels as safe or unsafe.

Skill #5. Recover and Replenish. *(Self-care)* Learn to rest and use the joy air pump to refill our tires.

Skill #4: Return to SCC

Regulating the Nervous System

Each of us was created hardwired with a system called the ANS (autonomic nervous system). Part of the ANS's job is assessing safety or danger cues and responding accordingly. Our senses continually take in information, our nervous system assesses the data and responds, and then we create a narrative that explains our experiences. We have no need to think about it; our body just automatically assesses, makes meaning, and reacts before that meaning becomes a conscious thought.

The ANS is an unconscious process, and much about it is outside of our control. We can learn to become aware of what state our ANS is in, however, and learn skills and strategies for shifting states more quickly. The quicker we are able to bounce back to a state of SCC after overwhelming emotions trigger the ANS, the quicker we will be able to return to the window of tolerance where we feel like ourselves, act like ourselves, connect easily with others, and feel a sense of well-being.

Three States of the Nervous System

For the purposes of this book, we will use a metaphor of a car for understanding the complexities of the nervous system. As with any metaphor, it does break down at points, but it's the simplest way to explain how the systems work.

The ANS nervous system works like a car. We have two main systems: the mobilization system, called the "sympathetic nervous system" (the gas pedal), and the immobilization system, called the "parasympathetic nervous system" (the brake).

Our nervous system also has several gears: drive, reverse, and park. The pedals do different things depending on what gear our system is in.

Drive: safe, calm, and connected. SCC is a relational system. When we perceive safety, we can feel safe, calm, and ready to connect. Because this state is relational and joy is developed in this state, we sometimes just refer to it as the joy state. In the joy state, we feel safe in the world, have people happy to be with us, and feel a sense of well-being. We have good "get up and go" (healthy stress). Our gas pedal and brake work together to form a healthy rhythm of "get up and go" and "rest and connect." Some stress is good. It gets us off the couch to do what needs done. In the drive gear, we feel productive. We also feel relational. Our relational circuits are on and we're ready to connect. Not all stress is good stress, however.

Overdrive or Reverse: fight-or-flight (sympathetic). Some stress switches our gear to overdrive or reverse. In this gear we have hyperarousal (a high-energy state), which might look like fight-or-flight where we feel emotions like fear, anxiety, and anger. Our ANS is always scanning the internal and external environment for safety or danger cues. If it detects danger, the ANS will automatically kick into the overdrive or reverse gear to solve the problem. It will dump stress hormones into the body to either fight or run. The main focus of this state is to get out of danger and find safety for ourselves and loved ones. In this state, our senses are heightened, our focus narrows to see only the problem that needs solving, our pupils dilate, and our body sweats.

Park: freeze or shutdown (parasympathetic). If I perceive that neither fighting or fleeing will solve the problem, the sympathetic nervous system falls back and the parasympathetic system takes over, putting the car in park. Shutdown is a state of hypoarousal, meaning it is a low energy state where the brake seems stuck. In this state, the person is shut down, depressed, disconnected, or dissociated. They may attempt to be small, invisible, and quiet, like an animal playing dead until the threat is gone. In this analogy, freeze would be when both pedals are stuck at the same time. The person feels frozen but inside their muscles are tense and full of energy.

It's important to recognize that all the gears are important for effective driving, but it's unhealthy to get stuck in overdrive, reverse, or park for too long. The good news is that we can learn skills to help us move back into the optimal state.

Self-regulation and Co-regulation

In her book, *The Polyvagal Theory in Therapy,* Dana goes into great detail about the nervous system, coregulation, and why connection is a biological imperative: it's how our nervous system learns to regulate. First, a caregiver regulates for us (external regulation), then our system learns to co-regulate with another person's help, and then we learn to self-regulate. We can exercise our nervous systems to build self-regulation muscles. This should happen naturally as a parent and child do life together, but sadly, many children do not have that gift. This gap in development can leave the brain/body without the regulation skills necessary to bounce back from adversity.

Learning emotional regulation happens on the fast track (faster than conscious thought) without our conscious engagement. As parents and caregivers, we can support this learning process by partnering with it, learning skills to aid the process, and practicing those skills with our kids.

The most important way to teach regulation is to be regulated yourself. When a baby cries, a parent attunes to the baby's cry, knows the baby well enough to know what the baby needs, picks the baby up, comforts the baby by meeting the need and soothing, and helps the baby return to joy. Over time, the baby will learn to co-regulate with the parent's nervous system.

The more often this road is traveled, the better and quicker the baby's brain and body can travel the path. As the child develops, he will learn to self-regulate his own emotions automatically.

It's worth noting that we will never outgrow our need for co-regulation. This is a beautiful part of being human: the power of presence. Our ongoing need for co-regulation explains why the difference between suffering and trauma is whether or not we feel alone in it. We were created to need God and each other. We will always benefit from being with another. Relational connectedness with God and others creates joy, and joy is what helps us endure suffering well. The joy of the Lord is our strength (Nehemiah 8:10). The author of Hebrews tells us that Jesus endured the cross "for the joy set before him" (Hebrews 12:2). He knew the relational joy that waited for him on the other side. God is the only one with infinite capacity. We cannot do life well in our own strength.

What happens when we go through overwhelming events and we feel alone? When overwhelming experiences are not metabolized and integrated and when we do not have another to help us process the pain, the sensory information and narrative store in the body as shattered pieces of a puzzle. The good news is that it is never too late to go back and complete the work. God is in the business of healing.

Bringing Awareness to the Nervous System's Definition of Safe and Not Safe

Learning to recognize what state (fight, flight, or freeze) our nervous system is in helps to integrate our sensory data with the story that we're telling ourself. Also, recognizing what triggers us to FFF will help us more easily navigate back to SCC.

The state that we're in profoundly affects the story we tell ourself. For example, if our ANS detects danger and puts us in danger gear, we may tell the story that we're not safe and the world does not feel safe. We may find it hard to navigate the day. Navigating school and other common activities is far more difficult when we're stuck in FFF (fight, flight, or freeze). The danger gear is great for backing out of situations that require it, but driving through our day backward is difficult and exhausting. It makes normal focus anything but normal, as in this story of a little girl written from the perspective of her adult self:

> *I sat frozen in my chair. The teacher was looking straight at me. Danger signals started ringing in my ears. I couldn't hear what she was saying.* What am I supposed to be doing? *I tried to read her face to see what she wanted from me. She looked frustrated.* I'm so stupid, why am I always so stupid? What did I miss now? *I looked around the room trying to see what the other kids were doing.* Oh, okay, get my book out. What page is everyone else on? Why do they always know what to do? Why am I always so lost? Be still and look at the page. Maybe she will forget about me and I can melt down into this chair and disappear from the room.

Unfortunately, this can be how children with trauma feel in school every day. They are exhausted and much gets missed. We can help them by learning to identify when they are off-line in FFF, and instead of treating their behavior like a discipline problem, we can send safety cues to their nervous systems, make eye contact with them, take deep breaths, and ask mindful questions that give their nervous system a chance to quiet and recover.

While each gear serves a purpose and is there for survival, we don't want to get stuck in survival mode. For children who have had trauma, they can get their gears stuck in reverse or park. Reverse helps us get out of the driveway, but if you have ever tried to drive backward you know how challenging it can be. Children driving backward through their day may look just like the other children while sitting quietly at their desks, but their brains are not processing what is happening in the classroom because their nervous systems are on high alert or shutdown. If they are in FFF, they are hearing every drip from the faucet and are distracted by every sight and sound in the room. Their brains are not online, so learning new things is difficult if not impossible. As a result, these children either sit quietly, trying to avoid bringing attention to themselves, or they struggle to keep themselves in the chair at all.

Every person must identify for themselves what feels safe and what feels scary and how the body responds to each. We can learn to attune to our ANS and feel the subtle shifts in our state to give us clues as to what our ANS perceives as safe and dangerous. Facial expressions, heart rate, the sensations in our throat, pupils dilating, sweating, and feeling cold can all be examples of the ANS moving into FFF. A change in tone of voice, gestures, posture (slouching, crossing arms in a protective manner, bowing up in an aggressive posture) can also indicate that we're moving between states.

To illustrate how the ANS responds to a danger cue, imagine you are standing behind a piece of glass and I throw a dodgeball at your face. You would flinch. Even though you consciously knew the ball couldn't hit you because you were behind the glass, your ANS would assess danger and throw you into reverse gear. Our emotional brain can respond in ways that don't always make sense to our thinking brain. But when we learn to read our emotional brain better, we can learn ways to better calm the emotional brain.

Danger Cues

What my nervous system perceives as dangerous could be different than yours. It largely depends on our experience. What's scary for me is not necessarily scary for you. For example, men with mustaches could become a danger cue if a person had a traumatic experience involving a man with a mustache and their nervous system never uncoupled mustaches from danger.

Safety Cues

Gratitude and deep breaths are two of the best ways to send safety signals to our nervous system, prompting it to turn off the alarm bells and return to SCC. My husband's hugs, my children's laughter, snuggles with my family, or my dog on the couch all signal to my nervous system that I am safe and can now enjoy connection with others. Smiles are powerful safety signals, and sitting in nature (especially near a body of water) is also a great safety signal for me. My nervous system relaxes, and I do my best thinking and connecting in those moments.

Self-Regulation

We discussed in Chapter 3 the power of retraining the brain for gratitude and connection. Learning to bounce back to SCC from overwhelming emotions is called self-regulation. Children who have had trauma are often not very good at regulating their emotions. Self-regulation requires that we have safe, regulated adults to learn from.

I was driving in the car the other day with my son. He was super anxious about being late for practice. Being late is one of his biggest triggers. I could see that his system was moving into fight-or-flight as we rounded the corner to our destination. I gently put my hand on his back between the shoulder blades (a spot known to help calm the nervous system), took a deep breath, and said, "It is going to be OK, buddy, I love you. Even if you are late, you will be OK."

This is an example of what it looks like when an adult who is able to stay regulated under stress is able to loan their nervous system to a person who is feeling dysregulated and co-regulate with them. There have been times when my children's strong emotions have dysregulated me and instead of calmly reacting as an external regulator, I exploded with frustration and said, "Get in the car, we are going to be late." Dysregulation can be contagious. Without the skills to combat it when we are with someone who is dysregulated, we are very prone to fall into dysregulation ourselves.

Connecting with others can sometimes feel overwhelming, depending on your experience with relationships. Pets and animals can help people learn to find safety in connection. Each person can experiment with what their nervous system likes best.

A simple tool for reversing fight-or-flight is by recalling three things you are thankful for and taking three deep breaths. When you or someone you are helping do this, you will most likely see a big shift. This is because the nervous system will take in both gratitude and deep breathing as signals of safety. The goal is for the brain's relational circuits to come back online.

Listen for a sigh or a yawn—these are good signs that a person's system is beginning to regulate.

Tools for Teaching Self-Regulation

Van der Kolk explains in *The Body Keeps the Score* that there are two ways to calm the ANS after the alarms have triggered: from the top down, using the PFC (prefrontal cortex), or from the bottom up, using breathing, movement, and touch. Dr. Karyn Purvis teaches that you can calm the ANS by engaging the senses. The following information is an attempt to give you ideas for sensory-engaging activities that will help your children and the children you work with learn to calm.

Children with a wide window of tolerance will be able to handle greater extremes of arousal. Children who have had trauma will have a narrower window. When you notice that a child in your life is starting to dysregulate, you can ask a heart-connection question. This only works if the child still has access to their thinking brain. We call this process "grounding."

Grounding Questions

Grounding questions work by helping us to become present to where we are in time and space and then become present with our own heart. You can ask something like, "What color are the chairs we are sitting in?" "Let's count how many colors can we see in the room," or "Let's play I Spy." You can also stop and do a body check-in. This is when the parent or caregiver asks children to notice where their feet are and wiggle their toes. They then move up the body, noticing different parts and engaging different muscles until they reach the top of their head. "Can you stretch your calf muscles? How about your belly muscles and your arms? Wiggle your arms. Stand up and stretch like you're trying to reach the ceiling. Wiggle your nose."

By now there should be engagement and smiles. If you think the children are ready, you can ask a question that helps them check in with their emotions. I teach that emotions are the language of the heart. They are how our heart communicates with us. I often use the language, "How's your heart?" to help children check in with what their heart might be saying to them that day. You can ask questions like, "How is your heart feeling right now?" or "What is happening in your heart right now?" Grounding questions help an individual return to the present and become aware of what he or she is feeling in the moment.

However, if you determine that the child no longer has access to their thinking brain, here are some other strategies you can try.

Children who are dysregulated no longer have access to their thinking brain. Do not try to reason with them. They can't hear you. You can, however, help to engage their senses:

What Are the Seven Senses?

We frequently talk about having five senses. These five are the senses we commonly mention when we talk about engaging with our physical world (touch, taste, smell, sight, and hearing). But we also have two other ways of receiving sensory data: our vestibular sense and proprioception.

Five Senses: Touch, taste, smell, sight, hearing.

Two Additional Senses: Vestibular: Involves the inner ear and controls equilibrium and balance. Proprioception: Affects movement and our sense of where we are in space. Developed through deep touch.

Engaging the Senses

Breathing *(younger children):*

- ☐ Soup analogy: Smell the soup, blow on the soup.
- ☐ Blowing bubbles: Kids love blowing bubbles and bubbles are very easy and inexpensive to find. We like to give each child their own container of bubbles. We then teach them that the same breath that makes the best bub-

bles also helps calm our bodies down: deep, long, and steady.

Breathing *(older children):*

- ☐ Three-count breathing: Breathe in through the nose for three counts, hold the breath in your lungs for a three count, gently blow your breath out for a three count, hold your lungs empty for a three count.
- ☐ Breathing with a ball: Have your children lay on their back. Count for them as they breathe in for three seconds, hold for three seconds, and blow out for three seconds. Once they are able to track with your counting, then place a ball on their belly and have them notice it rise and fall.

This kind of intentional breathing sends signals to the whole body that it is safe and can calm down. It helps the whole brain learn new pathways.

Remember, we have these beautiful things called mirror neurons. This means that as you take deep breaths and talk in a quiet, soothing voice, the mirror neurons in the child's brain will fire to mirror yours. The child's brain will then send the message to the body that it is safe to calm down.

***

Deep touch: We know the importance of touch. It's a physiological need. We know that babies without touch will not thrive. All kinds of brain development occur through deep touch. When children have been starved of touch, they may need more of it in order to catch up developmentally.

Examples: (1) Wearing a weighted blanket. (2) Gentle squeezing of the hands and arms starting at the wrist and moving up to the shoulder. (3) If they are willing (and it is culturally appropriate), give them a big hug, or let them sit in your lap.

These things send messages to the ANS that they are safe and their bodies will start to calm down. You may hear them take a deep breath. This is a good sign.

***

Movement: Get the body moving.

Examples include: running, pushing (push on the wall for a full sixty seconds), pulling (hold an adults hands and lean back, pulling on their arms), jumping jacks, jump rope, using the restroom (if you have been sitting for a while then take a bathroom break), go for a walk.

***

Eating or drinking: Eat a snack, drink water, suck on a sucker, chew gum.

***

Listening to music: Listen to any favorite or calming music.

Singing along is very powerful, especially with worship music.

***

Smelling essential oils: Lavender oil is a favorite, but there are many calming blends.

***

Keep in mind that after the initial calm down, it can take twenty to thirty minutes for the stress hormones to burn off. This is where exercise or a tool called a "sensory box" can help.

I help facilitate a resilience day camp every summer. One summer we had a little girl named Hope.[18] The first day of camp, Hope got triggered during the drop-off while saying goodbye to her mom. She became very upset. She refused to participate in the group activities. She would not engage with the staff at any level. As the morning progressed, Hope seemed to be escalating into a state of dysregulation. She was sitting in the back of the room crying. A staff member was sitting next to her, but she refused to talk.

I decided it was time to try sensory engagement and see if we could calm her nervous system back down. I walked over and put a bottle of water and some fruit snacks down in front of her. I then sat down next to Hope and, without saying a word, I began to take deep breaths. I was hoping that her nervous system would take the safety cues from mine. She quietly picked up the snack and ate it. I noticed her crying stop. She was then able to start looking around the room. I met her eyes with a smile. Within five minutes, Hope was calming down, and twenty minutes later she was running around with the other

---

18 Name and details changed.

children, participating in the group activity. I smiled when I heard her tell her mom at the end of the day that she had made a new friend.

Sensory Box

A sensory box is another way to provide children with high-sensory-engaging activities. A sensory box can be used in two ways:

1. It can be a tool for self-calming. (It might have been helpful for Hope as she sat there calming down.)
2. It can be presented as a high-sensory activity to help fill in the developmental gaps caused by a lack of sensory input in early childhood.

Sensory input is the primary way that infants learn to experience themselves and the world. Trauma disrupts this process. The more a child is exposed to different sensory experiences, the more information the brain will gather and the better the brain will be able to perform sensory motor tasks. This process is essential in learning to self-regulate.

Making a sensory box: Have your kids help make a sensory box during activity time. Have it sit in a special place for when the child needs/wants it as a self-calming strategy. TBRI suggests offering a "time in" instead of a "time out." This is a time for the child to sit close to a caregiving adult and engage in a high-sensory activity.[19] They could choose to have a weighted blanket on them as well.

Many kids with trauma have sensory-processing difficulties. They

---

[19] Strategy offered in Purvis, Cross, and Sunshine, *The Connected Child*, 101–102.

may be sensory seeking, which looks like hyperactivity. They may jump, spin, swing, or have trouble sitting still. Or they may be sensory avoidant: They don't like and avoid certain foods and textures. They don't like bright lights, loud or repetitive sounds, or getting their hands dirty. Part of the process of discovery with children is trying different things. Experiment with them. What do they like? What do they not like? Give the children choices as to which sensory experiences they want to include in their sensory box. As they explore, they will learn what works for them.

It can be helpful to expose children to different strategies for coping with their emotions and different self-calming strategies. As they experiment with what they like and don't like, they will gain new tools for self-regulation.

Quieting Exercises

These two exercises bring awareness to the nervous system.

Goals:

- ☐ Bring awareness to the nervous system.
- ☐ Learn skills to regulate. (If emotions are running too high, how do we calm down? If too low, how do we get moving again?)
- ☐ Introduce different coping and calming techniques.

Engine check (Alert Program®). Discuss how the nervous system works like a car engine. Blue is running too low, red is running too hot, but green is just right. When we're running in the green zone, we're our best self, we feel like ourselves, and we act like ourselves. We give the vehicle just enough gas to get up and go and just enough brake to calm and rest.

If we're running too hot, we may be feeling like our gas pedal is stuck to the floor. We're revving our engine and spinning our wheels. There's too much stress and we can't rest. If we're running low, our brakes may be stuck. We can't get up and go or get it done. We may want to shut down and not live at all.

Checking in with how the children's engines are running brings them awareness to the state of their nervous system. Then we can teach them the skills to regulate by practicing gratitude, breathing, grounding, and co-regulation.

***

Body check: Stand up. Notice your toes, feel them on the floor, and wiggle your toes. Now notice your legs, wiggle your legs, and jump around a bit. Now notice your back and shoulders and arms. How do they feel? Is there any tension in them? Squeeze and hold for five seconds. now shake it all out as in hokey-pokey. This can be a fun energy release and also helps the child learn to check in with themselves and release tension from their body.

Building Bridges Activities

Calming, body awareness, and self-regulation

Journaling: Grounding memory. *(Materials include pen and paper.)* I would like to invite you to actually write this out because writing engages both hemispheres of the brain and will be more powerful for you. Ask the Lord to remind you of a time you felt safe, calm, and connected. You might define the time as a time you felt at peace or a general feeling of "all is well," "I am loved," or "the world feels safe." Not everyone can remember a time and that is OK. You are not alone. You can just use your imagination to imagine what safe, calm, and connected would feel like.

Now remember or imagine what the weather was like. What did it feel like on your skin? What do you notice with your senses; the sights, smells, and sounds?

Next, I want to invite you (only if you are comfortable) to check in with your body. Notice how you feel as you are remembering this appreciation. Notice your breathing. If you are holding tension in your body, where do you feel it?

***

Discussion: Rehearsing a grounding memory. Discuss a time you felt safe, calm, and connected. What does it feel like when you are feeling overwhelmed? What can we do to return to SCC after feeling intense emotions?

***

Art Directives: Island of connected and safe vs. island of chaos and overwhelm. *(Materials include paper and pencils, colored pencils, markers, or crayons. A template has been provided, but you can always let the kids draw the islands.)* Have the children think of a time they felt safe. Ask them if anyone was with them or if they were alone. Ask them to close their eyes and remember what it felt like to be there. If they cannot think of a time they felt safe, have them imagine what it would feel like. Allow the children an opportunity to be in this place for a minute or two. Then pass out paper, crayons, and markers and have them draw their safe place.

Now, have the kids remember a time they felt triggered, fearful, or overwhelmed. Have them draw that on an island.

Next, have the children draw a bridge from the overwhelm island to the SCC island and write their self-calming tools on the bridge. Examples of self-calming tools could be hugs, deep breaths, hot baths, exercise, going for a walk with a friend, art, music, looking through an appreciation journal, or rehearsing gratitude.

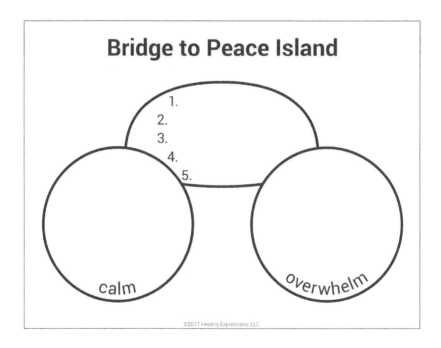

Skill #5 Recover and Replenish

This skill helps us learn to rest and use the joy air pump to refill the air in our tires.

Self-Care

I had four children in a five-year span, so the preschool years were intense. I remember sitting on the floor one night crying out to the Lord for help. My joy was gone; I was exhausted. I knew something was just not right, but I didn't know what. I am a reader and researcher. I am wired to identify a problem and then scour resources to find answers. The problem was that I wasn't finding answers. But the Lord heard my cry. He began to teach me. I realized that I was living in a state of overwhelm. I had to find ways to better manage my stress. At first, I tried adding good things to my life, like reading more books, doing Bible studies, and creating schedules. These things were good and helpful, but not enough.

Then, I heard the Lord say a simple word to my heart: *Rest*. Well, I didn't really know what that meant, so I started to study rest and sabbath and asked questions like, "How am I supposed to rest with four young kids?" What God has shown me over the years is that rest comes from secure attachment with him, which works like an anchor for the soul. I can learn to partner with this rest by taking multiple breaks during the day to attune to God's heart in gratitude. This reminds my spirit, soul, and body that he is still with me and I am loved.

Multiple times during the day I will stop, take a moment to quiet, breathe deeply, and enjoy the beauty of what is in front of me. Instead of worrying about yesterday or being anxious about tomorrow, I will take a deep breath and focus on something good today. This grows my ability to enjoy the day and increases my joy and the joy in my home. I become less and less stressed and more and more grateful. My kids and I will stop to admire a fish or a bird while on a walk. We will stop and listen to the sounds of nature or enjoy the cloud formations or a beautiful sunset. I have learned to savor the giggles and sounds of children playing. Essentially, my family is learning to walk in a rhythm of joy building and rest.

As previously mentioned, children need hours of face-to-face, eye-to-eye contact each day to grow their joy centers. This means mom and dad sitting on the floor playing games with the children, making eye contact, and delighting in each other. My busy and distracted life system was actually stealing my family's joy. Learning to slow down, pay attention, be intentional, and enjoy the moment has been one of the greatest gifts I ever received.

Feeling overwhelmed is a part of life, but we don't have to live there. We know that connections create joy and joy gives us strength. But sometimes connecting can be hard. For some of us, these skills are as easy as breathing, but for others they require intentional cultivation.

We can get trapped in a schedule without margin, running from event to event or meeting to meeting while never stopping to even check in with ourselves. Many Americans are running on very low joy. They have a continuous, slow leak and are headed toward a flat.

I learned quickly that there were things essential to keeping my capacity bubble inflated. As a therapist, I was hopping from client to client and then racing home to be there when my kids got home, starting dinner, and diving into the after-school routine. I hit a wall. I found that I was no longer able to be fully present with anyone because I had too much clutter in my head. I needed to start taking better care of myself. I could not be a good mom if I was not taking care of my own physical, mental, and spiritual needs. I built exercise, rest, and time with Jesus into my daily routine. I learned to eat better and take care of my physical well-being as well as my relational, emotional, and spiritual health. We are complex beings. Always changing. What worked for me when the kids were young is different from what works for me now.

For me, this has been a journey of building my emotional capacity so that I don't get overwhelmed as easily, and when I do, I've learned to bounce back quicker. It really is like an immune system. The stronger our immune system the less we get sick, and even when we do get sick, we recover quicker.

Learning to quiet, cultivate appreciation, and form healthy joy bonds builds our emotional capacity. Our capacity can go up and down from the daily stresses of life. When our joy bucket is low, we need each other. These same neuropathways that we use to connect with others are the ones we use to connect with God. But if we form fear bonds instead of joy bonds with our parents growing up, it can be hard for us to feel as though God is ever happy to be with us.

What refuels you, inspires you, and inspires gratitude? No two people will have the exact same answers. It takes exploration and time to figure out what depletes us and what fills us back up. It could be art, music, hot baths, the lake, the beach, hiking mountains, time spent with friends, time spent alone with a good book, learning new things—the list is endless. Try new things, and when you do something that feels life giving, make a note of it. Learn to journal the gratitude moments. It helps to reinforce all the feel-good chemicals, hormones, and neurological firings, and it also trains your mind to think on things that bring you joy.

The Power of Rest and Appreciation to Keep Us Bouncy

Appreciation is like a muscle that grows with training. We know from the Word of God and neuroscience that what we focus on will grow. We can train our brains to focus on things that are good, pure, and lovely, or we can train our brains to focus on what is wrong, scary, and bad.

When our brains are wired for danger or problems, it can feel impossible to find the good in anything. I have a friend who comes from a terribly sad childhood. She has experienced much abuse and trauma in her short life. Her brain is always scanning her environment to find the bad and scary and anticipate the next crisis. Because of this, she will often misread situations.

For example, if I use a particular word or give her a particular look, she will assume that I am mad at her and then worry about me rejecting her as a friend. One of the things we do together is look for things that are good, beautiful, and praiseworthy. We will appreciate the small wins in her life together, like beautiful weather so she was able to get out and take a walk. I often point out ways that I see God moving in her life. Her brain isn't trained to see those things, but mine is.

One day, my friend called me and reported with great joy that she could see God working in her life that day. She told me the story and said, "That was God wasn't it?!" What a blessing it was for me to get to watch her eyes open to God working on her behalf. She told me that day was the first time she ever believed God loved her. Her brain was learning to attune to the good things and not just ruminate on the bad and scary.

Here's another example of a time when appreciation changed *my* attitude and state of mind:

One night after the kids had gone to bed, I was walking up the stairs and I noticed these cute little dirty handprints on the wall. Now this was not the first time that day I had seen these prints. In fact, just hours earlier I had been very frustrated at those same marks because I had just repainted. The first time I saw them, I was overwhelmed from the stresses of the day and wanted to scold my kids because all I saw was the work those prints would require to fix.

But this time, as I looked at those little hands, I was overwhelmed with gratitude. My husband and I had just had a few hours of quiet reconnecting after a long week. I knew that one day not far from then, I would miss those adorable prints. I would miss taking those precious little hands in mine as we crossed the street or bowed to pray. I would even miss the dirty ones that lined my staircase because they meant that my precious children had been there that day, and it was good.

Because I found time to quiet my heart and mind from the day, I was able to return to joy, and appreciation followed. Appreciation is essential to living with joy.

How can we build appreciation? Worship, journaling each day about how you see God working, and any other practice that rehearses gratitude. I love to photograph nature and compile photos of things that bring me joy. When I see something that moves me or that I find beautiful, I will stop, take a picture, and appreciate it. I find that my brain is now trained to pick up on beauty from nature. I am catching hummingbirds, cardinals, cloud formations, sunrises, and sunsets more and more often.

Try this fun activity with children: Stop and notice the leaves on the sidewalk and count how many colors you can find. See if you can spot a turtle or fish in the pond. Find pictures in the clouds. These are ways to practice refilling our bounce throughout the day so that we stay bouncy.

Check-In Activity

This is an activity that is helpful as a teaching tool to educate children on how to "check in" with themselves. It's also a helpful way for the facilitator to "check in" with the children throughout the sessions.

Engine Speedometer (Alert Program®):[20] *(Materials: paper plates, paint (optional), card stock paper or any thick paper, markers, and brads.)*

---

20   *Leader's Guide to the Alert Program® for Self-Regulation* (Albuquerque, NM: TherapyWorks).

(See program manual for colored diagrams)

Discussion: Our bodies work like the engine of a car. They get us where we need to go. We need both a gas pedal and a brake. We need the gas pedal to get up and go and the brake to slow down and rest. Our bodies also need food, water, sleep, love, and connection to run well. Situations can cause our engines to run too low (for example, not enough of the good things we need) or rev too high (something has us worried or scared). Brainstorm with the kids what causes us to run too high or low. Also brainstorm what we can do when we feel too low (snap our fingers, go for a walk) and what things we can do when we feel too high (any of the self-calming strategies).

Directions: Have the children write their names on the bottom of the paper plate. Then with paints or markers, they can fill in the three colors at the top to indicate too cool (blue), just right (green), or too hot (red). Cut an arrow out of the card stock (or thick paper) and attach in the middle of the plate with a brad as an indicator arrow.

Summary Review

Let's stop and summarize what we have talked about so far. Trauma happens when we fall outside of our emotional capacity. This means that what we're experiencing feels like more than we can handle. Children are especially susceptible to trauma because they have not yet developed emotional capacity. The good news is that no matter how old you are, you can build more emotional capacity. As your emotional capacity grows, your children will have more capacity from which to borrow. This will build the neuropathways in their brains to help them bounce back from stress, growing their resilience. We can retrain the brain for appreciation and joy, which increases our ability to bounce back and even bounce forward from adverse situations and emotions.

Packing our kids in bubble wrap is not a sustainable solution. They *will* experience adversity and trauma in life. But what we know from research is that often the difference between stress and trauma is whether or not a person feels alone in it. Coming alongside a person in crisis mitigates the long-term effects of the event on the person. Imagine how powerful it could be as a parent, grandparent, teacher, or caring adult if you could learn to come alongside a child in times of adversity and lend them your PFC and emotional capacity so that they would have more resources for navigating the ups and downs of life. This is how we build bounce in our children.

Chapter Six

Power of Story

Children are excellent observers but terrible interpreters. When my kids were little, I would ask them, "What did you just hear me say?" or "What messages did you just get from that exchange?" I was often surprised by how they interpreted the world around them.

If your children have experienced abuse or neglect, then chances are their interpretation of what happens to them on a daily basis is filtered through a different lens than yours. They may have learned that connection is unsafe. They may feel unsafe talking about how they are feeling with you. Your first step is to build trust and establish authentic connection. Trust-Based Relational Intervention (TBRI®) resources are helpful for creating trust and connection between you and your child. I have included this website from the Karen Purvis Institute of Child Development in the resources list.

Purvis teaches that you can help build and support a child's ability to connect by providing a high-structure, high-nurture, and high-sensory environment where the child can begin making healthy connections with others. The TBRI model builds connection in three main ways: healthy touch, eye contact, and playful engagement. When presented in the context of play, the child will learn the skills twenty times faster.

Sense of Coherence

Sense of coherence speaks to one's ability to make sense of his or her world. Does my life make sense? Is it predictable or chaotic? When the unexpected happens, can I still believe that things are going to be OK? Do I believe that things generally tend to work out? Having a sense of coherence includes developing a world view, feeling like we belong to something bigger than ourselves, and believing that life has meaning and purpose. Story work is an excellent way to build a sense of coherence.

"Story work" refers to both telling and hearing a story. The stories can include personal narrative, reading a book, watching a movie, or making up stories in the imagination. All story work is helpful for building and supporting a child's ability to make sense of their world.

Education on Sense of Coherence for Primary Caregivers

Siegal and Bryson, in *The Whole-Brain Child*, discuss the importance of storytelling for the integration of traumatic memory into a narrative that makes sense. Because children are excellent observers but terrible interpreters, they need to borrow an adult's PFC (prefrontal cortex) to make sense of what they see. Below is an example of how storytelling can be helpful in processing trauma.

You may have noticed that children like to tell stories over and over again. They also like to ask the same questions repeatedly. They tell and retell the story to make sense of what has happened. We can help them do this. When something unexpected happens in the life of a child, we can help them process what happened by helping them tell the story. By doing so, we lend them our PFC and we help build pathways in their brain to return to love and safety. If we get in the habit of doing this with the "little t traumas" in our children's lives, they grow strong in it and then it will be easier for them to do in the "big T traumas."[21]

Here is an example of a "little t trauma" and what it looks like to tell the story. Let's say your child falls down and gashes his leg on something sharp. Lying in bed that night, you might engage your child in some storytelling by saying something like this:

Do you remember when you fell this morning? Remember when Mommy ran to you and picked you up, and then we got a towel and put it on the cut? It hurt to put the towel on the cut, but we had to do it to stop the bleeding, and then we called the doctor. The doctor told us to go to the hospital so that the doctors could put stitches in your cut to help it to heal better. Do you remember the doctor's funny mustache? It moved up and down when he talked. And do you remember

---

21   Siegel and Bryson, *Whole-Brain Child*.

the picture of the cute little puppy on the wall that we looked at while we waited for the doctor to come back in? What do you remember about today?

Telling the story like this, including both the traumatic and the ordinary events from the day, helps the child to integrate all the pieces of the story. Each time you tell the story, you are helping the child integrate the emotions, sights, smells, and sounds into a narrative that can be told. The child learns, "I can experience adversity, feel my emotions, talk about it with people who care about me, return to love and safety, and go to bed peacefully in my bed at night."

Much of this work happens naturally just by doing life together. We don't have to think about it. For example, when a child experiences a thunderstorm and runs into their parent's bedroom, the parent may comfort them by saying, "I know it sounds scary." The parent may lend the child their PFC by saying something like, "Even though it sounds really loud, the storm can't hurt us. It's outside, and we are safe inside." The parent may let the child lie down with them until they have calmed back down. By doing this, the parent helps the child to name their feelings and organize the feelings into words that give meaning and context to their experience. Also, by offering comfort, the parent helps the child navigate a pathway back to feeling safe, calm and connected.

When a process like this happens, children learn they are not alone. They have people in their life who will love them and support them. They can fall down, get hurt, be comforted, and get back to life as they know it. The world doesn't end.

What happens if a child is unable to make sense of trauma? What if the child's emotional brain can't piece together the pieces of the story? Unresolved trauma will store in the body in fragmented parts. The child will have trouble fitting the parts together in a way that makes sense. Sometimes a child's mind will try to make sense of them, but the result is irrational. For example, the child may develop a fear of men with mustaches because the emotional brain associated the fear of sitting in the doctor's office with the doctor's mustache. The more we can talk to our children and help them to make sense of what is happening around them, the more they will be able to integrate their emotional brain and rational brain. They will learn to regulate their own emotions and make sense of their experiences in the future. The Whole-Brain Child is an excellent resource for learning more about using story to help children process the challenges of life.

Adults with Unresolved Trauma

Unfortunately, many of us have scenes from our story that are still unresolved. Maybe we lacked someone able to help us make sense of the story, or maybe the scene was so horrific that there were no answers to the questions we had. If you know you have unresolved childhood trauma, I recommend walking through your story with someone. There is a tremendous amount of research coming out about the power of storytelling in healing and becoming more resilient. Talk to a friend, counselor, or pastor. Participate in a group designed to help people unpack their stories. Your story is worth telling, and you are worth being heard.

Hope and Optimism

Hope and optimism are super important in resilience research. Models like Positive Psychology and the Snyder Hope Theory have extensively covered this ground.[22] It is clear from the research that optimistic people are more resilient. In fact, entire resilience models have been rooted in hope and optimism. I know—I can hear you pessimists and realists out there rolling your eyes at me. I'm sorry, but it's true. Optimism is rooted in our belief system; it's the lens through which we see the world. According to the Cambridge Dictionary, "optimism is the tendency to be hopeful and to emphasize or think of the good parts in a situation rather than the bad parts, or the feeling that in the future good things are more likely to happen than bad things." Hope from the resilience research is defined as having the ability to set goals, make a plan, and work the plan.

Our experiences and the conclusions we draw from our perspectives determine how we interpret the world around us and what we decide is true. We are always filing away our experiences as "evidence." If we have a bank full of evidence showing that God is good, faithful, and dependable, then we have faith. If, however, we have an evidence

---

[22] See C. R. Snyder, *Handbook of Hope: Theory, Measures, and Applications*, (Cambridge, MA: Academic Press, 2000); K. Keune and C. L. Sheridan, *Interrelationships of Stress Resistance Factors in Predicting Health*, at Annual Meeting of the American Psychological Association, San Francisco, CA, 2001; Keune and Sheridan, *Resilience, Coping Styles, Expressiveness and Health: Toward an Integrated Framework*, at Annual Meeting of the American Psychological Association, San Francisco, CA, 2002.

bank full of abandonment stories, terrible experiences, and feeling alone in the world, then we will see the world through a broken lens.

As parents, we can lay the groundwork through healthy attachment and appreciation to help our children have an optimistic view of the world that says, "God and the people I love are going to be there for me when I need them." Whenever we experience God's faithfulness, or someone we love attuning to us and walking with us through a difficult situation, a deposit is made into our evidence bank that builds trust. Ultimately people will let us down, but God never will. We may not always feel him working, but as we collect life experiences in our evidence bank of God's faithfulness, our belief system will shape around the understanding that, "God is faithful and will walk with me through every fiery trial." The emotions will follow.

Jesus Is Our Hope

What story do we believe? Our overall attitude and hope come from the stories we believe.

As believers, we put our hope in Jesus. He is our plan.

Jesus has gone before us and made a way for us. Not only does he guarantee our hope for the future, but he is our hope for today. He came to heal the broken hearted and set the captive free. Hope is an essential element of the Christian life. It is anchored in Jesus.

"The Spirit of the Lord is on me, because he has anointed me to proclaim good news to the poor. He has sent me to proclaim freedom for the prisoners and recovery of sight for the blind, to set the oppressed free, to proclaim the year of the Lord's favor" (Luke 4:18-19).

Which story are you living? Is it a scary story of doom and destruction or a grand love story of redemption? The story you believe will greatly impact your ability to endure suffering and bounce back from adversity.

I want to stop and say I have compassion for the many believers who struggle to fully embrace the love story of God. Many believers believe the Bible with their minds, but their hearts seem to tell a different story. I was one of them. Because of trauma I experienced as a child, my head, heart, and nervous system could not agree on which story we were living.

Experiential Lenses

We are meaning makers. We are wired to take in data from our world (make observations), find the meaning of the data (interpret it), and draw conclusions based on our interpretations (apply it). Over time, these conclusions become generalized and develop into a lens through which we interpret our experiences. The problem is, many of us have drawn our conclusions based on faulty interpretations because of poorly formed lenses.

The Bible offers hope for this problem. Romans 12:2 tells us to be transformed by the renewing of our minds. 2 Corinthians 10:5 tells us to tear down anything that sets itself up against the knowledge of God and take captive every thought to make it obedient to Christ. This speaks to me of the importance of believing rightly. Taking our thoughts captive, tearing down lies, and believing truth.

Professionally as a Christian counselor and personally in my own life, I have learned how experience is often more powerful than words. I can tell someone God loves them and that he has never left or abandoned them. But if they have "evidence" that tells a different story, they will look at me and say, "I want to believe that. I know that's the correct Sunday school answer, but something in me is screaming that it's a lie." They will then tell me all the ways that they felt alone and abandoned when terrible and unjust things happened to them.

After my own healing journey and twenty-five years of walking with people through the healing process, one thing I know for sure: Jesus is willing to enter into any story. He is able to guide people out of the dark prison of fear and into the light of his redemptive love, changing their narrative forever. I have seen clients invite Jesus into the most painful places of their stories, the very places where belief systems were most broken and—in many cases—the place where their faulty belief systems were born. In every case, Jesus spoke truth to their hearts and met them in an experiential way that melted away their belief in the Devil's lies. Because of the work Jesus did, their false beliefs were replaced with truth.

Hope and optimism flow from our attachments. If we have secure attachments, then it's easy to believe that the world is generally safe and that we might have to work hard and be adaptive, but things usually have a way of working out. Even in times of trouble and difficulties, we learn that life is basically good, and we learn to see problems as solvable. When we feel safe and connected, we develop optimism and hope. Hope takes this belief one step further and makes a plan: 1) we can set goals, 2) we have a pathway to meet those goals, (3) we can work hard to achieve those goals, and (4) we can be flexible when challenges hit and adjust our goals and plan.

The more we practice these skills, the more automatic they become and the stronger our hope. Going back to the analogy of when I moved to a new town and was learning my way around, the first several times I drove I had to think hard and pay attention. But after a while it became second nature. I didn't have to think about finding my way, I just knew. The same is true anytime we learn new things and forge new pathways in the brain.

Making a Hope Plan

Help children learn optimism and create pathways to building hope.

Discussion: What does the word "hope" mean to you? What do you think of when you hear the word "optimism?"

Define hope and optimism. Explain as discussed just previously: The difference between optimism and hope is that optimism is an attitude and hope is a plan. Optimism is the basic belief that we might have to work hard and be creative, but things have a way of working out. Even in times of trouble and difficulties, we believe that God is bigger than my troubles and is able to work all things together for good, and we learn to see problems as solvable. Hope takes this belief one step further and makes a plan: (1) we can set goals, (2) we have a pathway to meet those goals, (3) we can work hard to achieve those goals, and (4) we can be flexible when challenges hit and adjust our goals and plan.

Hope is an important part of resiliency. Hope is more than optimistic thinking. Hope is taking optimistic thoughts and developing a plan to get where we want to go. We are going to practice this in the next exercise.

Hope exercise (steps we're taking): Draw your own two feet on a piece of paper. On the left foot, write one or two goals. On the right foot, devise a plan to achieve the goal. Discuss how plans often change, and that's OK. We can stay flexible, reassess, and rework the plan as we go.

Purpose

Purpose is a very powerful tool for building hope. Helping children identify their strengths and the traits that make them unique, creating a plan for cultivating their gifts, and delighting in them when they use the gifts God wired into them are all good ways to help a child build hope and purpose.

The Heart's Story

The Bible teaches that we are born into a world at war. The kingdom of light and the kingdom of darkness have been at war from the beginning of time. God created humanity for the display of his splendor. We were created to be in fellowship with and to worship our Creator. However, because we are created in God's image and are the crown of his creation, we have an enemy. This enemy is out to kill, steal, and destroy all that God has done and is doing.

Satan is the great deceiver, and he set out from the beginning of time to deceive man into sin. In the garden, man began listening to this enemy and believing his lies. Because of man's great fall into sin, we are now in bondage to things of death and destruction.

Here is our hope: Jesus came into this broken and fallen world to restore his people and set us free from the bondage of sin and death (Isaiah 61:1–3). God says he will give us a new heart and put a new spirit in us. He will remove from us the heart of stone and give us a heart of flesh (Ezekiel 36:26). 2 Corinthians 5:17 says, "Therefore, if anyone is in Christ, the new creation has come: The old has gone, the new is here!" This is called redemption.

The young heart will receive many assaults to its wholeness. Assaults come at the heart not only as a result of our own brokenness and poor choices, but also because of the brokenness of the people in our lives and the state of the world in which we live. We must not forget that we have an enemy who understands the importance of the human heart, and even after our salvation, he seeks to keep the human heart in bondage and blind to the victory won by Christ on the cross.

Christians can be saved but at the same time continue to be bound by lies and unbelief that come from a wounded heart. The enemy of our souls wants to keep our hearts captive so that the church is left benign and unable to fight, or left unaware that the battle rages and therefore powerless in it. Paul tells us to abide in the power of Christ and the victory won at the cross, and to put on the armor of God, pick up our weapons, and fight (Ephesians 6:16–17). 2 Corinthians 10:3–5 says,

> *For though we live in the world, we do not wage war as the world does. The weapons we fight with are not the weap-*

ons of the world. On the contrary, they have divine power to demolish strongholds. We demolish arguments and every pretension that sets itself up against the knowledge of God, and we take captive every thought to make it obedient to Christ.

The object of this great war is the human heart, but the battlefield is the mind. The consequences of a wounded heart are addiction, despair, and a life lived only to survive. But Jesus came to set the captive heart free and redeem it to victory and power. Jesus came to bring us life. Only he can heal our hidden wounds. We, however, can learn to take captive our thoughts by identifying lies we believe and replacing them with God's truth. Romans 12:2 says, "Do not conform to the pattern of this world, but be transformed by the renewing of your mind. Then you will be able to test and approve what God's will is—his good, pleasing, and perfect will." Our inheritance is a life of victory and freedom. This is the glory of God. This is why he came. Jesus came that we may have life, and have it abundantly.

The Key to Heart Connection

Could it be that the key to becoming fully alive is a heart fully alive, awake, and free? The heart is where we connect with God. It's where we plug into the power source. It's the spring from which life flows. No wonder Satan has worked so hard to keep man's heart bound in woundedness. If God's people are running from their pain, then they will stay disconnected from their hearts.

So how do we connect with our hearts? As in the very best of fairytales, love is the key that unlocks the human heart and wakes it up from its slumber.[23] We love because God first loved us (1 John 4:19). Our journey to abundant life begins with understanding his love for us. Then, we can learn to love him with all of our heart, soul, mind, and strength. As Jesus's love begins to awaken the heart, we discover that the heart is a very complicated place, often harboring old wounds that never healed. A person may not even know when they were wounded but only that they live with feelings that cause discomfort or debilitating pain.

Wounds often give birth to lies. These lies become such a part of the person's thinking that the person may not even know they believe a lie. As Jesus shines his light into the dark places of the heart, however, these lies are exposed. He replaces the lies with truth and heals the wound. This is why he came. He came to heal the broken heart and set it free.

Trauma shatters the soul. Jesus picks up the pieces, breathes resurrection life into our inner most places, and makes us whole. Healing is the work of Jesus, but telling our story is how our brain integrates all of what it experiences. There is power in our story.

Why Story?

We have overcome by the blood of the lamb and the word of our testimony (Revelation 12:11).

---

23   John Eldredge, *Waking the Dead: The Glory of a Heart Fully Alive* (Nashville: Thomas Nelson, 2006).

Story is a powerful tool in our healing process and in building faith. As we are able to organize our experiences in meaningful ways, we see God at work in our lives.

Every day, we are flooded with many thoughts, feelings, experiences, and pieces of sensory data. Our ability to organize all of this input into one coherent story helps us make sense of our lives and what happens to us.

Story is one of the best ways to make neurological connections in the brain. Story, unlike anything else, engages the right and left hemispheres of the brain (horizontal integration). It also integrates vertical connections in the brain. I believe this neurological integration is what makes movies and books so powerful for us. It may also be why Jesus taught in parables. Transformation and renewing of the mind are about so much more than obtaining the truth. The truth—Jesus himself—must be firmly planted in our hearts and belief systems. And we must be firmly rooted in his love.

When we tell our story, we are able to connect with the many pieces and parts of ourselves and our experiences, bringing it all together and connecting our story to God's big story.

Each of us has a story. Our stories are all part of the big God-story. We cannot escape pain and suffering on our journey, but our suffering can have meaning. God is able to bring beauty from ashes. He takes what the enemy means for evil and works it for our good.

We can let Jesus restore and redeem our story. We no longer need to be trapped in a tale of despair and hopelessness. Our God can bring beauty from ashes, good from evil, light from darkness, life from death, victory from defeat, and truth to a heart hardened by lies. "Those who sow in tears will reap with songs of joy. Those who go out weeping, carrying seed to sow, will return with songs of joy, carrying sheaves with them" (Psalm 126:5).

Reframing: The Stories We Tell Ourselves (Aligning with Truth)

When my son was in the first grade, he came home from school one day and announced that he was terrible at basketball. I asked him where he got that idea. He responded quite confidently that he had played basketball in his PE class and he was terrible. I asked him if he had ever played basketball before.

"Well, no," he said.

"Then how do you know? Wouldn't it be more accurate to say you don't have the skills yet? And that maybe if you go to a few practices with a coach you could learn how to play?"

"Well, I guess," he conceded.

"Then let's reframe the story you told yourself and make it a bit more true."

The stories we tell ourselves have a great impact on our perception and the emotional cocktail that gets released in our bodies.

We get to choose the narrative that we rehearse in our mind. Whichever one we choose to focus on will impact us on every level. Every day is a choice. Whichever story we rehearse will solidify and become part of our neurology. It's like walking a path in the woods. The more we walk the path, the more well-worn it becomes and the easier it becomes to walk it. Which GPS system will you follow to create your path? Love or fear? The Bible tells us to be transformed by the renewing of our minds. It also tells us to take every thought captive and make it obedient to Christ.

Growing Love, Pulling the Weeds

Taking thoughts captive

Discussion: Not every voice we hear in our head is our voice. God talks to us through our mind and so does the enemy. (If you are not ready to have this conversation about the enemy with your child, then just say that not every thought we have is true.) When we learn to hear God's voice, then we will know when the enemy is whispering lies to us. We can also learn to identify shame messages that we are believing. We can learn how to reject lies and focus on truth.

***

Define self-talk: How we talk to ourselves is important. After you make a mistake, do you talk to yourself about the mistake the same way you would talk to someone you care about who made the same mistake?

***

Gardening metaphor *(activity for younger children):* We are like plants. What does a plant need to grow up healthy? Rich soil, water, and sunshine. We need to be careful what we put in our soil. Toxic words and lies can make us feel sick just like they can make a plant sick. These are like weeds in a garden; we can learn to pull them out and throw them away.

***

Journaling: Take it captive *(activity for older children and adults)*. What does God say is true about me? Ask God, take time to listen, and see what you hear. Read scripture together. Ask Jesus to reveal to you or show you what the truth is. It can be helpful to discuss the ways God talks to us. Sometimes he talks to us through the Bible, sometimes we just hear a word in our mind, like "loved," and sometimes we may see a picture, like a daddy holding a little girl. Or we may just have a knowing in our heart. This would look something like "I just feel his love for me, and I know he is saying, 'I love you.'" The key is to ask, does this word, picture, or "knowing" line up with what the Bible says is true? If it does, then it's safe to say it's from God. All good things are from God and all things from God align with scripture.

Write down what God says and rehearse it. Hang it on the wall. Thank him for it every day. We want it to grow in our heart and minds.

Next, ask Jesus to show you places where you have made agreements with the enemy. What lies of the enemy have you agreed with? Lies often come in the form of a shame message, things like, "You are ugly, stupid, worthless, or unlovable."

Replace the lie with the truth by speaking out loud: "I reject the lie,_____, in Jesus name. I come out of agreement with it today and choose to embrace the truth_____."

Story Work

Discussion Questions
- What is your favorite movie?
- Who was your favorite character and why?
- What are obstacles that the main character faced?
- How did they overcome?

- Watch a movie or read a story together and talk about it. Discuss what they liked or didn't like about the movie. Identify the obstacle in the story and how the characters overcame. Recognize how our favorite characters often have personal obstacles to overcome, including the Big God Story.

***

Art Directive: Story Map. *(Materials include paper and pencils, colored pencils, markers, or crayons.)* Explore a map together with your child/children. Now allow them to create their own map. This map tells a story. They can tell their own personal story, borrow one, or make one up. Identify the main character and include three obstacles that the main character must overcome. The children can create a key to help tell the story. Each child will identify challenges on their map such as mountains, valleys, rivers, and caves. The children can come up with creative ways of getting around each challenge. For example, Indiana Jones uses his whip to swing over the river. The children can use real life solutions or their imagination. Heroes can be given special gifts or super powers. This directive is very empowering for the child, especially if they are struggling with powerlessness.

As you watch movies and read books together, you can continue to ask these questions. Read scripture together, too. There you will find many examples of God's faithfulness. When your family faces a challenge, pray together for God to give you a plan for overcoming the obstacle. When you see answered prayers, thank him together.

Chapter Seven

Some Joy Before You Go

Life is hard. We will each experience many ups and downs in our lifetime and so will our children. The good news is that Jesus has already overcome them on our behalf. All good stories have obstacles to overcome and a love to win. The Big God Story is the ultimate love story. We have the gifts of being fully loved and never alone, and we know the end of the story: God wins. This is our hope as believers.

Jesus is our ultimate hope because he provided us with a pathway to healing our deepest wounds, overcoming sin, and defeating death. Jesus is also present to walk with us each and every day as we journey through life's ups and downs. He is good at helping us find pathways that lead to the abundant life and joy. We may get scared or lost, but God is always with us and walks with us just as we walk with our children through their highs and lows.

The Bible tells us that what we focus on is important. Our world view and how we see the world shapes us in many ways. We can learn to focus on the truth—truth that is both the person Jesus and his Word. We can also train our brains to focus on what is good and pure and lovely. We can build strong muscles of appreciation and joy.

Our children are bombarded with lies every day. The world, the flesh, and the Devil are obstacles to running the race well. We can teach our children to throw off everything that hinders and entangles them and run with perseverance. We can teach them to take their thoughts captive, reject lies, rehearse what is true, and run the race that they have been given to run. We can teach them to fix their eyes on Jesus who modeled for us enduring suffering by fixing our eyes on the joy that is to come. *See Philippians 4:8, Romans 12:2, Hebrews 12:1–3, and 2 Corinthians 3:3–5.*

We can learn skills to help us connect well, navigate adversity well, and live with more joy. We can teach those skills to our children. But ultimately the only one who has infinite capacity is the one who created us. When we connect to the vine that is Jesus, we tap into life. The greatest gifts we can offer our children are pathways that lead to God. He is the only parent who loves perfectly, connects perfectly, leads perfectly, and disciplines perfectly.

I pray that this book has provided you a few new resources and pathways for building connections with God that offer both joy and peace and for teaching those skills to your children so they may also know the joy, peace, and love of their Heavenly Father.

Resources for Further Study

The Bible

Emotional Capacity/ Emotional Maturity
>Marcus Warner and Stefanie Hinman, *Building Bounce*
Friesen, Wilder, Bierling, Koepcke, and Poole, *Living from the Heart Jesus Gave You*, a Life Model book
Marcus Warner and Jim Wilder, *Rare Leadership*

Emotional Healing:
>Marcus Warner, *Understanding the Wounded Heart*

Resilience:
>Positive Psychology
Resilient Schools Initiative by Hinman and Foster

Spiritual Warfare
>Marcus Warner, *Spiritual Warfare*
Neil Anderson, *Bondage Breaker and Steps to Freedom in Christ*

DID/SRA: Contact me for a more extensive list
>Melissa Finger, Seek First Ministries: Understanding Trauma Coping Systems

Trauma
>Dr. Bessel van der Kolk, *The Body Keeps the Score*
Francine Shapiro, EMDR resources
Deb Dana, *The Polyvagal Theory in Therapy*

Trauma and Children
    Daniel Siegal and Tina Payne Bryson, *The Whole-Brain Child*
    Karyn Purvis, *The Connected Child*
    Donna Jackson Nakazawa, *Childhood Disrupted*
    TBRI Institute, website: child.tcu.edu

Shame and Vulnerability
    Dr. Curt Thompson, *Anatomy of the Soul; Soul of Shame*
    Dr. Brené Brown, *Gifts of Imperfection; Rising Strong; Braving the Wilderness*

Made in the USA
Coppell, TX
03 May 2023

16404310R00089